97 Delicious Custard Recipes: A Sweet Treat for Every Occasion

Custar Trea

Contents

INTRODUCTION

Welcome to 97 Delicious Custard Recipes: A Sweet Treat for Every Occasion! We are so thrilled you have chosen to explore the delicious world of custard. Custard is a classic, creamy and delicious dessert that has been enjoyed for centuries. In this cookbook, you will find 97 recipes for a refreshing and indulgent treat that you can enjoy any time.

Custard is a classic dessert that is both creamy and full of flavor. With its sweet taste, it's perfect for any occasion. It can be served for breakfast, for a snack, for an afternoon treat, or as a light dessert. No matter when or where you choose to indulge, you will be sure that it will be a hit!

In this cookbook, we've curated 97 of the most delectable custard recipes on the planet. From classic custard pies and custard puddings to modern variations like crème brûlée, custard tarts, and frozen custard desserts. Each recipe is given detailed instructions, along with helpful tips and tricks along the way. You can easily customize each one to desired serving sizes and sweetness levels.

Whether you want a quick and easy dessert to serve at a dinner party, a decadent mid-week treat, or a fun way to introduce your kids to cooking, this cookbook is sure to provide plenty of inspiration. We've thought of every occasion, so you're sure to find the perfect custard recipe to fit the occasion.

What better way to say luxury than with a silky smooth custard? Light, creamy, fragrant and sweet, custards are the perfect treat for any occasion. Whether you're a novice baker or a pro in the kitchen, the 97 recipes in this cookbook offer something for everyone. So get ready to be inspired.

We hope you enjoy all the delicious custard recipes in this cookbook. Let us know your favorites, share them with friends and family, or bookmark them for later. Happy baking!

1. Vanilla Bean Custard

Vanilla Bean Custard — Enjoy a delicious treat with this creamy, smooth, and decadent vanilla bean custard. This classic dessert can be prepared and served in just about an hour.

Serving: 4 - 6 | Preparation Time: 10 minutes | Ready Time: 50 minutes

Ingredients:
* 1 cup whole milk
* 1 cup heavy cream
* 1/2 cup granulated sugar
* Scraped seeds from 2 vanilla beans
* 1/2 teaspoon Kosher salt
* 4 egg yolks

Instructions:
1. Preheat the oven to 325F.
2. In a medium saucepan, heat the milk, cream, sugar, vanilla beans, and salt over low-medium heat until the sugar is dissolved and the mixture is almost simmering.
3. In a medium bowl, whisk together the egg yolks.
4. Slowly pour 1/2 cup of the heated cream mixture into the bowl and whisk until fully incorporated.
5. Whisk the egg mixture into the saucepan with the remaining cream mixture.
6. Cook over medium-low heat for about 8 minutes until the custard has thickened, whisking continuously.
7. Pour the custard through a fine-mesh sieve into a large bowl.
8. Divide the custard among 4-6 ramekins.
9. Place the ramekins in an oven-safe baking dish and add enough water so it comes halfway up the sides of the ramekins.
10. Bake for about 30 minutes until the custards are just set.
11. Allow the custards to cool to room temperature and then chill in the refrigerator for at least 2 hours before serving.

Nutrition Information (per serving):
Calories: 176 kcal; Fat: 10 g; Saturated Fat: 6 g; Carbohydrates: 16 g; Protein: 4 g; Sodium: 166 mg; Fiber: 0 g; Sugar: 15 g

2. Chocolate Custard

Chocolate Custard is a creamy, indulgent dessert that is perfect for those looking for an extra special treat. It is simple to make with only a few ingredients and requires minimal effort for maximum deliciousness.

Serving: 8. | Preparation Time: 15 minutes. | Ready Time: 40 minutes.

Ingredients:
- 2 cups milk,
- 4 egg yolks,
- 1/4 cup sugar,
- 3 tbsp cocoa powder,
- 1/4 tsp salt, 2 tbsp butter,
- 1/2 tsp vanilla extract.

Instructions:
1. In a small bowl, mix the egg yolks, sugar and cocoa powder until creamy.
2. In a medium saucepan, heat the milk, salt and butter over low heat. Do not boil.
3. When the milk is hot, slowly add the egg yolk mixture while stirring.
4. Cook over low heat, stirring constantly, until the mixture thickens.
5. Remove from the heat and stir in the vanilla extract.
6. Pour the custard into individual custard cups or serving dishes. Let cool to room temperature, and then chill in the refrigerator for at least 30 minutes.
7. Serve chilled.

Nutrition Information: Calories: 198; Total Fat: 12g; Saturated Fat: 6g; Cholesterol: 134mg; Sodium: 160mg; Total Carbohydrate: 17g; Dietary Fiber: 1g; Sugar: 13g; Protein: 8g.

3. Berry Custard

Berry custard is a delicious and creamy dessert that combines fresh berries with a creamy custard base. This easy-to-make recipe is perfect for entertaining and crowd-pleasing!

Serving: 6-8 | Preparation Time: 10 minutes | Ready Time: 50 minutes

Ingredients:
• 2 cups of fresh berries (e.g. raspberries, blueberries)
• 2 cups of heavy cream
• 3/4 cup of granulated sugar
• 5 large eggs
• 1 teaspoon of vanilla extract
• Pinch of salt

Instructions:
1. Preheat oven to 350 degrees Fahrenheit.
2. In a medium bowl, combine cream, sugar, eggs, vanilla and salt and whisk until the mixture is smooth.
3. Grease a 9-inch baking dish with butter.
4. Place the berries into the baking dish and top with the custard mixture.
5. Place the baking dish into the oven and bake for 45-50 minutes or until the custard is set.
6. Serve chilled.

Nutrition Information (per serving):
• Calories: 340
• Fat: 24g
• Protein: 7g
• Carbohydrates: 23g

4. Lemon Custard Tart

Lemon Custard Tart is a classic and easy to make treat, bursting with a tangy lemon flavor and creamy custard-like texture. It's an ideal alternative to classic lemon meringue pie and is sure to please the whole family.
Serving: 8 | Preparation Time: 15 minutes | Ready Time: 1 hour and 15 minutes

Ingredients:
- 1 9-inch tart crust
- 1 cup granulated sugar
- 4 large eggs
- 1/4 teaspoon salt
- 1 cup fresh lemon juice
- 1/2 cup butter, melted

Instructions:
1. Preheat oven to 375F.
2. In a medium bowl, whisk together the sugar, eggs, salt, and lemon juice.
3. Slowly whisk in the melted butter until mixture is smooth.
4. Place the tart crust on a baking sheet. Pour the lemon custard mixture into the tart crust.
5. Bake in preheated oven for 45 minutes, or until golden brown and a toothpick inserted in the center comes out clean.
6. Let cool completely before serving.

Nutrition Information (per serving): Calories 227, Total Fat 15g, Saturated Fat 9g, Cholesterol 76mg, Sodium 116mg, Carbohydrates 21g, Fiber 0g, Sugar 14g, Protein 3g

5. Caramel Custard

This Caramel Custard is an absolute indulgence! This creamy and delicious snack or dessert will satisfy and delight your sweet tooth.

Serving: 4 | Preparation Time: 15 minutes | Ready Time: 60 minutes

Ingredients:
- 2 cups of whole milk
- 2 tablespoons butter
- 1 cup of granulated sugar
- 5 large egg yolks
- 5 tablespoons of caramel sauce

Instructions:
1. In a saucepan, heat the milk and butter until warm.
2. In a bowl, whisk the egg yolks and sugar together until light and creamy.
3. With a ladle, slowly add the warm milk mixture to the egg and sugar mix, stirring continuously.
4. Pour the custard mix into four individual ramekins.
5. Place the ramekins in a baking tray.
6. Fill the tray with boiled water until halfway up the sides of the ramekins.
7. Bake in the preheated oven at 350F/180°C for 60 minutes.
8. Allow to cool.
9. Drizzle with caramel sauce.

Nutrition Information (per serving):
Calories – 359
Fat – 19.1 g
Carbohydrates – 39.3 g
Protein – 6.9 g

6. Coconut Custard

Coconut Custard is a creamy and sweet dessert perfect for special occasions. It blends fragrant coconut milk with eggs and sugar, then bakes to perfection.

Serving: 6-8 | Preparation Time: 10 minutes | Ready Time: 30 minutes

Ingredients:
- 2 13.5-ounce cans full fat coconut milk
- 3/4 cup granulated sugar
- 4 large egg yolks
- 1 teaspoon vanilla extract
- 1/8 teaspoon salt

Instructions:

1. Preheat oven to 350F (177°C). Grease a 9-inch pie dish with butter or nonstick spray.
2. In a medium saucepan, combine coconut milk and sugar. Bring to a simmer and cook for 2 minutes until sugar is dissolved, stirring frequently.
3. In a medium bowl, whisk together egg yolks, then slowly whisk in the coconut milk mixture until combined. Add vanilla and salt and stir to combine.
4. Pour the mixture into the prepared pie dish. Bake for 25-30 minutes until the edges are lightly browned and set.
5. Cool for 15 minutes before serving.

Nutrition Information:
Serving size: 1/8 of recipe (145g)
Calories: 250, Fat: 15g, Saturated fat: 13g, Carbohydrates: 22g, Fiber: 0g, Sugar: 16g, Protein: 3.6g, Sodium: 161mg.

7. Creme Bralee

Creme Bralee is a sweet and creamy custard with a crunchy caramelized sugar topping. It is the perfect romantic dessert to serve to your loved one.

Serving: 4-6 | Preparation Time: 10 minutes | Ready Time: 1 hour

Ingredients:
- 3 cups heavy cream
- 3/4 cup granulated sugar
- 8 large egg yolks
- 1/2 teaspoon vanilla extract
- 1/2 teaspoon salt
- 1/2 cup turbinado sugar (for topping)

Instructions:
1. Preheat oven to 325F.
2. Heat cream and 3/4 cup sugar in a medium saucepan over low heat, stirring occasionally until the sugar dissolves. Remove from heat and set aside.

3. In a bowl, beat the egg yolks until light in color.
4. Gradually beat in the cream mixture into the eggs until well blended.
5. Stir in the vanilla and salt.
6. Pour mixture evenly into 6 - 7 ramekins and place in a roasting pan with 1 inch of hot water.
7. Bake for 40 - 50 minutes or until custard is set.
8. Remove from oven and let cool, then refrigerate for at least 4 hours or overnight.
9. Just before serving, sprinkle sugar evenly and as much as desired over the custards.
10. Place custards under broiler for about 5 minutes until sugar is caramelized.
11. Enjoy!

Nutrition Information: Per Serving (based on 6 servings) Calories: 350, Fat: 25g, Saturated Fat: 15g, Cholesterol: 250mg, Sodium: 230mg, Carbohydrates: 25g, Fiber: 0g, Sugar: 23g, Protein: 5g.

8. Banana Custard

Banana Custard is an irresistible dessert that combines sweet and creamy custard with chunks of ripe banana for a delectable treat. This easy to prepare dish is sure to satisfy any sweet tooth and is perfect for a special occasion or gathering.

Serving: 6 | Preparation Time: 15 minutes | Ready Time: 1 hour

Ingredients:
- 3 cups of whole milk
- 3 large ripe bananas, peeled and diced
- 3/4 cup of white sugar
- 2 tablespoons of all-purpose flour
- 1/4 teaspoon of salt
- 2 tablespoons of butter
- 1 teaspoon of vanilla extract
Instructions:
1. Preheat oven to 350F (175°C). Grease an 8-inch square baking dish.

2. In a large bowl, combine the milk, sugar, flour, and salt. Stir until the sugar is dissolved and the mixture is creamy.
3. Add the butter and vanilla extract, and stir until everything is fully mixed.
4. Place the diced banana into the baking dish and pour the custard mixture over top.
5. Bake in the preheated oven for 30 to 40 minutes, or until the top is golden brown and the custard is set.
6. Allow to cool before serving.

Nutrition Information: Per Serving (1/6 of recipe): Calories: 273 Total Fat: 8.6g; Cholesterol: 20mg; Sodium: 199mg; Total Carbohydrates: 46.3g; Dietary Fiber: 1.3g; Protein: 4.7g.

9. Carrot Custard

Carrot Custard is an easy and delicious recipe. The bright orange color combined with the rich, creamy custard makes a great dish for breakfast, lunch, or dinner. It's a great way to use up those carrots you've got lying around, and is just as nutritious as it is tasty!

Serving: 8 | Preparation Time: 10 minutes | Ready Time: 50 minutes

Ingredients:
- 2 1/2 cups carrots, freshly grated
- 3 eggs
- 1 cup whole milk
- 2 tablespoons unsalted butter, melted
- 1/4 cup granulated sugar
- 1/4 teaspoon ground nutmeg
- 1/2 teaspoon ground cinnamon
- 1/4 teaspoon salt

Instructions:
1. Preheat oven to 350F.
2. Grease an 8-inch baking dish with butter and set aside.
3. In a large bowl, mix together the grated carrots, eggs, milk, melted butter, sugar, nutmeg, cinnamon, and salt.

4. Pour the mixture into the prepared baking dish and place it in the oven.
5. Bake for 40-45 minutes or until the custard has set.
6. Remove from oven and let cool for 10 minutes before serving.

Nutrition Information:
Serving size: 1/8 of recipe
Calories: 146, Total Fat: 6 g, Saturated Fat: 3 g, Trans Fat: 0 g,
Cholesterol 63 mg, Sodium: 90 mg, Carbohydrates: 18.5 g, Fiber: 1.2 g,
Sugars: 12.2 g, Protein: 4.3 g.

10. Maple Custard

This creamy, luxurious Maple Custard is a classic dessert that is both easy and elegant. Perfect for all occasions, you can enjoy it plain or with a dollop of whipped cream for a delicate finish.

Serving: 4 | Preparation Time: 15 minutes | Ready Time: 90 minutes

Ingredients:
• 2 cups of whole milk
• 2/3 cup of pure maple syrup
• 1 tsp of pure vanilla extract
• 3 large eggs
• 1/4 teaspoon of ground nutmeg
• 1/2 teaspoon of salt

Instructions:
1. Preheat oven to 350 degrees
2. In a medium-size bowl, whisk together the eggs, nutmeg, and salt
3. In a medium-size saucepan, heat the milk, maple syrup, and vanilla over medium heat. Bring the mixture to a boil and remove from heat.
4. Slowly incorporate the egg mixture into the maple mixture, stirring continuously.
5. Strain the custard through a mesh strainer and pour into four separate 6-oz. ramekins.
6. Place the ramekins into an oven-safe dish filled with 1 inch of water and place into preheated oven.

7. Bake for 30-40 minutes or until the centers are set.
8. Let cool for 1 hour before serving. Enjoy with a dollop of whipped cream.

Nutrition Information: 388 Calories; 18g Fat; 12g Carbohydrates; 7g Protein per serving.

11. Honey Custard

Honey Custard is an easy-to-make dessert that combines rich custard and the unmistakable flavor of sweet honey. The perfect balance of nutty and sweet flavors makes this a truly satisfying treat. Serve this Honey Custard as a light dessert after a special meal.

Serving: 6-8 | Preparation Time: 15 minutes | Ready Time: 30 minutes

Ingredients:
- 4 large eggs
- 3/4 cup sugar
- 2 cups heavy cream
- 1/3 cup honey
- 1 teaspoon vanilla extract
- 1/4 teaspoon ground nutmeg

Instructions:
1. Preheat oven to 350 degrees F.
2. Beat eggs and sugar together in a medium bowl until light and creamy.
3. In a separate bowl, stir together cream, honey, vanilla and nutmeg.
4. Add egg mixture to cream mixture and stir until combined.
5. Pour mixture into 8" greased baking dish.
6. Bake for 25-30 minutes, until custard is set.
7. Serve.

Nutrition Information: Calories: 267; Total Fat: 14.7g; Saturated Fat: 8.9g; Cholesterol: 127mg; Sodium: 30mg; Carbohydrates: 28.8g Fiber: 0.3g; Sugar: 28.3g; Protein: 4.3g; Vitamin A: 11.2%; Vitamin C: 0.2%; Calcium: 5.9%; Iron: 4.6%.

12. Orange Custard

Orange custard is a creamy, delicious dessert featuring oranges and custard. Perfect for any occasion, this delightful treat is sure to make your party guests smile!

Serving: 8 | Preparation Time: 10 minutes | Ready Time: 30 minutes

Ingredients:
- 1 cup orange juice
- 1/4 teaspoon orange extract
- 2 tablespoons sugar
- 2 cups whole milk
- 2 large eggs
- 1/4 teaspoon vanilla extract
- 1/4 teaspoon ground nutmeg

Instructions:
1. Preheat the oven to 350 degrees Fahrenheit.
2. In a small saucepan, bring the orange juice, orange extract, and sugar to a boil. Simmer over medium heat for 3 minutes, stirring occasionally. Take off heat and set aside.
3. In a medium bowl, whisk together the milk, eggs, vanilla extract, and nutmeg until well blended. Gradually add the hot orange juice mixture, stirring constantly.
4. Pour the mixture into an 8-inch baking dish. Place the baking dish into a larger baking dish filled with hot water. Bake for 25-30 minutes, or until the custard is set.

Nutrition Information:
Serving size: 1/2 cup
Calories: 114
Fat: 4.0g
Carbohydrates: 16.1g
Protein: 5.2g

13. Pistachio Custard

This creamy and sweet Pistachio Custard is a delectable dish that combines the nutty flavor of pistachio with the richness of custard. The result is an incredibly delicious treat.

Servings: 4 | Preparation Time: 15 minutes | Ready Time: 45 minutes

Ingredients:
-3 large eggs
-3/4 cup sugar
-3 cups whole milk
-3 tablespoons cornstarch
-1/4 teaspoon salt
-2 teaspoons pure vanilla extract
-2/3 cup shelled pistachios
-Additional shelled pistachios for garnishing

Instructions:
1. Preheat the oven to 350F.
2. In a medium bowl, whisk together the eggs, sugar, and cornstarch. Set aside.
3. In a large saucepan, heat the milk over medium-high heat. Once the milk is just below boiling point, slowly whisk in the egg mixture.
4. Reduce the heat to medium-low and cook, stirring constantly, until the custard thickens. Make sure to scrape down the sides of the pan to avoid scorching.
5. Remove the custard from the heat and stir in the salt, vanilla extract, and pistachios.
6. Pour the custard into a baking dish or ramekins. Place the dish or ramekins in a larger baking dish. Pour boiling water into the larger dish to come halfway up the sides of the custard dish or ramekins.
7. Bake for 30 minutes, or until the custard sets and the top begins to brown.
8. Let cool for at least 15 minutes before serving. Garnish with remaining pistachios, if desired.

Nutrition Information:
Calories: 414; Total Fat: 16.6g; Total Carbohydrate: 53.1g; Protein: 9.9g

14. Apple Custard

Apple Custard is a delicious, creamy dessert that combines the sweetness of apples with the richness of a simple custard. This easy to make treat is the perfect way to end a meal.

Serving: 8-10 | Preparation Time: 20 minutes | Ready Time: 1 hour

Ingredients:
-4 apples, cored and diced
-1/4 cup caster sugar
-1/4 tsp ground nutmeg
-1/4 tsp ground cinnamon
-1/4 cup water
-2 eggs, lightly beaten
-2 cups milk
-1/2 tsp vanilla extract

Instructions:
1. Preheat oven to 350F.
2. In a bowl, mix together the apples, sugar, nutmeg, and cinnamon. Place this mixture into an 8x8 inch casserole dish.
3. Add the water to the apples in the casserole dish and stir to combine.
4. In a separate bowl, whisk together the eggs, milk, and vanilla extract. Pour this mixture over the apples in the casserole dish.
5. Bake for 40 minutes, or until the center is set. Allow the custard to cool for 15 minutes before serving.

Nutrition Information (per serving): Calories: 153, Total Fat: 5g, Saturated Fat: 3g, Cholesterol: 55mg, Sodium: 71mg, Total Carbohydrate: 23.5g, Dietary Fiber: 1g, Protein: 6g.

15. Pumpkin Custard

Pumpkin Custard is a classic autumnal treat. Sweet and spiced, this custard takes pumpkin puree and combines it with milk, sugar, eggs, and other spices.
Serving: 8. | Preparation Time 10 minutes. Ready time 45 minutes.

Ingredients:
- 2 cups pumpkin puree
- 2 cups milk
- 4 eggs
- 1/2 cup of sugar
- 1 teaspoon of ground cinnamon
- 1/2 teaspoon ground nutmeg
- Pinch of ground cloves
- Pinch of ground ginger

Instructions:
1. Preheat oven to 350 degrees. Grease a 9-inch baking dish with butter.
2. In a large bowl, whisk together the pumpkin puree, milk, eggs and sugar until completely combined.
3. Add in the cinnamon, nutmeg, cloves, and ginger, and whisk until fully incorporated.
4. Pour the custard mixture into the greased baking dish.
5. Bake for 45 minutes until a knife inserted into the center of the custard comes out clean.
6. Allow to cool before serving.

Nutrition Information:
Serving Size: 1 slice
Calories: 125
Total Fat: 5g
Saturated Fat: 2g
Cholesterol: 70mg
Sodium: 39mg
Carbohydrates: 14g
Dietary Fiber: 1g
Sugars: 11g
Protein: 5g

16. Cinnamon Custard

Cinnamon Custard is a delicious, comforting dessert that is full of warm spices and creamy custard goodness. It is easy to make and provides a great way to top off a special meal.

Serving: 4 | Preparation Time: 15 minutes | Ready Time: 20 minutes

Ingredients:
- 3/4 cup whole milk
- 1/4 cup heavy cream
- 3 egg yolks
- 2 tablespoons sugar
- 1 teaspoon ground cinnamon
- 1/4 teaspoon ground nutmeg
- 1/4 teaspoon vanilla extract

Instructions:
1. Preheat the oven to 325 degrees.
2. In a medium bowl, whisk together the milk, cream, egg yolks, sugar, ground cinnamon and nutmeg.
3. Pour the mixture into four individual baking dishes.
4. Bake for 15 minutes or until the custards are just set.
5. Remove from the oven and let cool slightly before serving.

Nutrition Information: Per Serving (1/4 of recipe): Calories 200, Fat 12g, Saturated Fat 7g, Cholesterol 165mg, Sodium 65mg, Carbohydrate 17g, Protein 6g.

17. Rice Custard

Rice Custard is a dessert made with a combination of cooked rice, milk, and cream. Its creamy texture and delicate sweet flavor make it a delicious comfort food.

Serving: 4-6 | Preparation Time: 25 minutes | Ready Time: 1.5 hours

Ingredients:
- 3 cups cooked rice

- 1/2 cup granulated sugar
- 3 cups whole milk
- 2 cups heavy cream
- 1/4 teaspoon salt
- 1 teaspoon vanilla

Instructions:
1. Preheat the oven to 300 degrees F. Grease an 8-inch baking dish and set aside.
2. In a pot over medium heat, combine the cooked rice and sugar. Stir continuously until the sugar is dissolved.
3. Slowly add the milk, cream, and salt to the pot and mix. Stir with a whisk until the mixture is smooth.
4. Remove from the heat and whisk in the vanilla.
5. Pour the mixture into your greased baking dish.
6. Bake in the preheated oven for 1 hour and 15 minutes until the custard is set.
7. Let cool before serving.

Nutrition Information: Serving Size: 1/6 of recipe. Calories: 329, Total Fat: 15g, Saturated Fat: 9g, Cholesterol: 61mg, Sodium: 148mg, Total Carbohydrate: 41g, Sugars: 21g, Protein: 5g

18. Amaretto Custard

Amaretto Custard is an Italian-style dessert made of creamy, smooth custard infused with a hint of amaretto liquor. It is a great way to end a meal in a unique and flavorful way!

Serving: 5-6 servings | Preparation Time: 10 minutes | Ready Time: 2 hours

Ingredients:
- 2 cups whole milk
- 1/2 cup sugar
- 2 eggs
- 2 tablespoons all-purpose flour

- 1/4 cup amaretto liquor

Instructions:
1. Heat the milk in a saucepan over medium heat until it is just below boiling.
2. Meanwhile, in a bowl, whisk together the sugar, eggs, and flour until they are well blended.
3. Gradually whisk the hot milk into the egg mixture.
4. Pour the mixture back into the saucepan and cook over low heat, stirring constantly, until the custard thickens, about 5-10 minutes.
5. Remove the custard from the heat and stir in the amaretto liquor until combined.
6. Pour the custard into individual serving dishes and place in the refrigerator to chill for at least 2 hours.

Nutrition Information (per serving):
Calories: 210
Fat: 6g
Saturated Fat: 3g
Cholesterol: 76mg
Sodium: 33mg
Carbohydrates: 25g
Protein: 7g

19. Peach Custard

Peach Custard is a sweet, creamy, and lightly-spiced dessert that is sure to satisfy any sweet tooth. It's a perfectly balanced treat, combining the freshness of peaches with the comforting richness of custard for a flavor that is both delightful and indulgent. Serve it as a light accompaniment to a meal or enjoy it as a dessert.

Serving: 8 | Preparation Time: 20 minutes | Ready Time: 1 hour

Ingredients:
-3 cups peeled and diced fresh peaches
-3 tablespoons sugar
-3 eggs

-2 cups milk
-1/4 teaspoon nutmeg
-2 tablespoons butter
-1 teaspoon vanilla

Instructions:
1. Preheat oven to 350F.
2. In a large mixing bowl, combine the peaches and sugar.
3. In a separate bowl, beat the eggs and stir in the milk, nutmeg, butter and vanilla.
4. Pour the egg mixture over the peaches and mix to combine.
5. Pour the mixture into an 8-inch buttered baking dish.
6. Bake for 40 minutes or until a knife inserted in the center comes out clean.
7. Let cool for 10 minutes before serving.

Nutrition Information (per serving): Calories: 149; Total Fat: 6g; Cholesterol: 82mg; Sodium: 65mg; Total Carbohydrates: 18g; Protein: 5g; Fiber: 1g.

20. Rum Custard

This velvety and delicious Rum Custard is a traditional English dessert. It is made with just a few simple ingredients and is guaranteed to be a hit when served.

Serving: 4-6 | Preparation Time: 5 minutes | Ready Time: 45 minutes

Ingredients:
- 2 cups heavy cream
- 5 egg yolks
- 1/4 cup white sugar
- 2 tablespoons dark rum
- 1/4 teaspoon ground nutmeg

Instructions:
1. Preheat oven to 350 degrees Fahrenheit.

2. In a medium bowl, beat the egg yolks and sugar until the mixture is thick.
3. Slowly add the cream and rum, stirring constantly.
4. Grease a casserole dish with butter and pour the custard mixture into it.
5. Sprinkle the top with nutmeg.
6. Place the dish in the oven and bake for 40 minutes or until set.
7. Let cool slightly before serving.

Nutrition Information (per serving):
Calories: 410 kcal, Total Fat: 33 g, Saturated Fat: 20 g, Protein: 4 g, Carbohydrates: 19 g, Sugar: 12 g, Fiber: 0 g, Sodium: 59 mg.

21. Almond Custard

Almond Custard is a healthy and creamy dessert that combines eggs, cream, almond extract, and brown sugar for a delicious sweet treat. This dish is a great way to spice up the classic custard recipe.

Serving: 8 | Preparation Time: 10 minutes | Ready Time: 40 minutes

Ingredients:
• 4 egg yolks
• 2 cups heavy cream
• 1 teaspoon almond extract
• 1/3 cup packed light brown sugar

Instructions:
1. Preheat oven to 375 F. Grease an 8-inch pie pan with butter.
2. Beat together egg yolks, heavy cream, almond extract, and brown sugar in a bowl until combined. Pour the mixture into the greased pan.
3. Bake in preheated oven for 35-40 minutes or until a knife inserted into the middle of the custard comes out clean.
4. Allow the custard to cool; enjoy.

Nutrition Information:
Serving: 1 slice

Calories: 383 kcal
Carbohydrates: 15.6 g
Protein: 6.1 g
Fat: 33.7 g
Saturated Fat: 20.4 g
Cholesterol:220 mg
Sodium: 75 mg
Potassium: 75 mg
Fiber: 0.7 g
Sugar: 14.3 g
Vitamin A: 1498 IU
Calcium: 70 mg
Iron: 1 mg

22. Hazelnut Custard

Hazelnut Custard is a creamy and smooth dessert that is delectably indulgent and is sure to be a crowd pleaser.

Serving: 8 | Preparation Time: 10 minutes | Ready Time: 1-2 hours

Ingredients:
- 3 cups of whole milk
- 3 large eggs
- 1/2 cup of granulated sugar
- 1 teaspoon of pure vanilla extract
- 1/2 cup of chopped hazelnuts
- Pinch of salt

Instructions:
1. Preheat your oven to 350F and lightly butter an 8-inch baking pan and set aside.
2. In a bowl whisk together the milk, eggs, and sugar until they are fully combined.
3. Add in the vanilla extract, hazelnuts and salt and mix together until all ingredients are evenly distributed.

4. Pour the mixture into the prepared baking pan and place into the preheated oven and bake for about 40-50 minutes, until the custard has set.
5. Allow the custard to cool completely before serving.

Nutrition Information: per one serving of Hazelnut Custard contains approximately 260 calories, 11g fat, 32g carbohydrates and 8g of protein.

23. Lavender Custard

For something special, try this delicate, sweet and creamy Lavender Custard. With its pleasant floral taste, it makes for an excellent dessert or fancy breakfast dish.

Serving: 3 | Preparation Time: 10 minutes | Ready Time: 5 hours

Ingredients:
- 2 1/2 cups of heavy cream
- 6 large egg yolks
- 1/2 cup of sugar
- 2 teaspoons of lavender buds
- 1 teaspoon of vanilla extract

Instructions:
1. In a small saucepan, pour the heavy cream over the lavender buds and heat to just under a boil.
2. In a medium bowl, whisk egg yolks and sugar together until light and creamy.
3. Pour the hot cream slowly into the egg yolk mixture while whisking constantly.
4. Pour the custard mixture into small cups and cover with aluminum foil.
5. Place the custard cups into a large baking dish and fill the dish with hot water until it reaches halfway up the sides of the cups.
6. Place the dish into the oven at 325F and bake for 45 minutes.
7. Remove from the oven and let cool for a few minutes before transferring to the refrigerator.

8. Serve chilled and enjoy.

Nutrition Information:
Per serving:
Calories: 190
Fat: 16gCarbohydrates: 9g
Protein: 3g

24. Lime Custard

Lime Custard is a delectable dessert that combines the tartness of limes with the creamy sweetness of custard. It's an easy-to-make recipe that is perfect for summer gatherings or as a comforting after-dinner treat.

Serving: Makes 10 servings | Preparation Time: 20 minutes | Ready Time: 1 hour

Ingredients:
- 2 cups heavy cream
- 4 limes, zested
- 4 limes, juiced
- 1/2 cup sugar
- 5 egg yolks
- 1/2 teaspoon salt

Instructions:
1. Preheat oven to 350F. Grease 10 ramekins with butter.
2. In a medium saucepan over medium heat, warm the cream and lime zest until just warm.
3. In a medium bowl, whisk together the egg yolks, lime juice, sugar and salt.
4. Gradually add the warm cream mixture to the egg mixture, whisking constantly.
5. Pour the custard mixture into the ramekins and transfer to a baking dish.
6. Carefully fill the baking dish with enough hot water to come halfway up the sides of the ramekins.
7. Bake for 40 minutes or until custards are set.

8. Cool, then chill the custards in the refrigerator for at least 1 hour. Serve chilled.

Nutrition Information: Calories: 188 Carbohydrates: 15g Fat: 13g Protein: 4g Sodium: 215mg Cholesterol: 111mg

25. Apricot Custard

Apricot Custard is a light and creamy dessert that is perfect for special occasions. This delectable custard is made with fresh apricots, eggs and cream, giving it a sweet and tart flavor. With a little preparation and baking time, you can enjoy a delicious apricot custard that your guests will love.

Serving: 4 | Preparation Time: 20 minutes | Ready Time: 1 hour

Ingredients:
- 4 apricots, peeled and pitted
- 3 eggs
- 1/2 cup cream
- 1/4 cup sugar
- 1/4 teaspoon ground nutmeg
- 1/4 teaspoon ground cinnamon

Instructions:
1. Preheat oven to 350 degrees F.
2. Cut apricots into thin slices and set aside.
3. In a large bowl, whisk together eggs and cream.
4. Add sugar, nutmeg, and cinnamon and mix until fully combined.
5. Grease a 9-inch pie plate with butter and pour custard mixture into it.
6. Top with thin slices of apricots and gently press down into custard.
7. Bake for 40 minutes or until custard is set and golden brown.
8. Let cool before serving.

Nutrition Information:
Calories: 120
Fat: 6.2g
Carbohydrates: 12g

Protein: 4g

26. Rosemary Custard

Rosemary Custard is a deliciously creamy, unique twist on the traditional custard dessert. It has a hint of rosemary accents that makes it perfect for special occasions.

Serving: 6-8 | Preparation Time: 45 minutes | Ready Time: 2 hours

Ingredients:
-1 1/2 cups whole milk
-2 large eggs
-1/2 cup granulated sugar
-11/2 teaspoons minced rosemary
-1/4 teaspoon vanilla extract
-1/4 teaspoon ground nutmeg

Instructions:
1. Preheat oven to 350F (175°C).
2. In a medium bowl, whisk together the eggs and sugar until light and fluffy.
3. Slowly add the milk, rosemary, vanilla extract and nutmeg, stirring to combine.
4. Grease a 9-inch baking dish, pour the custard mixture into it, and bake for 45 minutes.
5. Remove from oven and cool in the refrigerator for at least an hour before serving.

Nutrition Information:
Per Serving (1/8 of the recipe):
Calories: 111 kcal, Carbohydrates: 14 g, Protein: 3 g, Fat: 5 g, Saturated Fat: 3 g, Cholesterol: 58 mg, Sodium: 42 mg, Potassium: 94 mg, Fiber: 0 g, Sugar: 12 g, Vitamin A: 237 IU, Vitamin C: 0 mg, Calcium: 68 mg, Iron: 0 mg.

27. Strawberry Custard

Strawberry Custard is a delicious and creamy dessert that is sure to satisfy even the most discerning sweet tooth. This recipe offers a fresh and luscious combination of sweet flavor with a creamy texture that is perfect for any special occasion.

Serving: 8 | Preparation Time: 10 minutes | Ready Time: 40 minutes

Ingredients:
- 2 1/2 cups fresh strawberries, sliced
- 3 large eggs
- 1/3 cup sugar
- 1 tablespoon all-purpose flour
- 1/4 teaspoon salt
- 3 cups half-and-half
- 1 teaspoon vanilla extract

Instructions:
1. Preheat the oven to 350F and grease a 2-quart baking dish with nonstick butter spray.
2. In a medium bowl, combine strawberries, eggs, sugar, flour and salt. Stir until everything is evenly combined.
3. Pour the mixture into the prepared baking dish and spread evenly.
4. In a medium saucepan over medium heat, heat the half-and-half and vanilla extract until hot. Pour over the strawberry mixture, stirring carefully.
5. Bake in the preheated oven for 40 minutes, or until the custard is set and a knife inserted into the center comes out clean.
6. Cool to room temperature and serve.

Nutrition Information: Calories: 193 Total Fat: 8g Carbohydrates: 22g Protein: 6g Sugar: 17g Sodium: 230mg

28. Cardamom Custard

Cardamom Custard is an exotic, flavorful and creamy dessert, made from only a few simple ingredients. This light, creamy and aromatic custard is the perfect way to end a meal or start a weekend brunch.

Serving: 4 servings. | Preparation Time: 10 minutes | Ready Time: 45 minutes

Ingredients:
- 2 cups whole milk
- 2 tablespoons sugar
- 2 tablespoons cornstarch
- 2 eggs
- 2 teaspoons ground cardamom
- 1 teaspoon vanilla extract

Instructions:
1. In a medium saucepan, heat the milk over medium-high heat until just simmering.
2. In a small bowl, whisk together the sugar, cornstarch, eggs, cardamom, and vanilla extract until smooth.
3. Slowly add the egg mixture to the hot milk, whisking constantly.
4. Bring the mixture to a simmer and cook, stirring constantly until the custard is thick and creamy, about 5 minutes.
5. Remove from heat and transfer the custard to a bowl.
6. Let cool before serving.

Nutrition Information:
Serving Size: 1/4 cup; calories: 126; fat: 5g; saturated fat: 3g; cholesterol: 78mg; sodium: 40mg; carbohydrates: 14g; fiber: 0g; sugar: 8g; protein: 6g.

29. Peanut Butter Custard

Peanut Butter Custard is a delectable, creamy, and smooth dessert that will tantalize your taste buds! Perfect for a special occasion or indulgent treat, this recipe combines the power of peanut butter and the richness of custard for a delightful mix of flavors.

Serving: This recipe makes 12 servings. | Preparation Time: 10 minutes. | Ready Time: Approximately 1 hour.

Ingredients:
- 2 cups of milk
- 2/3 cup of granulated sugar
- 4 egg yolks
- 3/4 cup creamy peanut butter
- 2 tablespoons of cornstarch
- 1/4 teaspoon of salt
- 1 teaspoon of vanilla

Instructions:
1. Preheat the oven to 350F and lightly grease a 9-inch round baking dish.
2. In a medium saucepan, heat the milk over medium-high heat until it just begins to boil. Reduce the heat to low and slowly add the sugar, stirring until dissolved.
3. In a medium bowl, whisk together the egg yolks, peanut butter, and cornstarch until fully combined.
4. Gradually add the hot milk-sugar mixture to the egg-peanut butter mixture while stirring constantly.
5. Return the mixture to the saucepan and cook over medium-high heat, stirring constantly, until the mixture thickens and begins to simmer. Remove from heat and stir in the salt and vanilla.
6. Pour the custard mixture into the greased baking dish and spread evenly. Bake for 20-22 minutes, or until the center is almost set.
7. Let cool at room temperature for 1 hour before serving.

Nutrition Information: Each serving of Peanut Butter Custard provides 300 calories, 18g of fat, 27g of carbohydrates, 7g of protein and trace amounts of sodium and cholesterol.

30. Mango Custard

Mango Custard is a classic dessert that can be used to bring an upbeat tropical flavor to your desserts! The mango custard is full of flavor, is easy to make, and will become a family favorite! It can be served for dessert, or as a special brunch dish.

Serving: 8 | Preparation Time: 10 mins | Ready Time: 30 mins

Ingredients:
- 2/3 cup of sugar
- 2 tablespoons of cornstarch
- 3 cups of whole milk
- 1/4 teaspoon of salt
- 4 egg yolks
- 2 teaspoons of vanilla extract
- 2 cups of diced fresh mango

Instructions:
1. Preheat oven to 375F (190°C).
2. In a large bowl, whisk together sugar, cornstarch and salt.
3. In a separate bowl, whisk egg yolks until light and fluffy.
4. Gradually add the sugar mixture to the egg yolks, whisking constantly.
5. In a medium saucepan, heat the milk until it boils.
6. Slowly add the hot milk, whisking constantly to the egg mixture.
7. Pour the mixture into a baking dish and bake for 15 minutes.
8. Lower the oven temperature to 350F (176C) and bake for another 15 minutes.
9. Remove from the oven and stir in the mango and vanilla extract.
10. Refrigerate for 2 hours before serving.

Nutrition Information:
Serving Size = 1/2 cup, 120 Calories, 2 g Fat, 24 mg Cholesterol, 62 mg Sodium, 22 g Carbohydrates, 1 g Protein.

31. Banana Cream Custard

Banana Cream Custard is an utterly delicious, creamy dessert that is sure to be a crowd-pleaser.

 Serving 4-6, this dish is ready in an hour, with a 15 minute | Preparation Time.

Ingredients:
- 4 Bananas
- 3 Tablespoons All-purpose flour
- 3/4 cup Sugar
- 2 1/2 cups Whipping cream
- 2 Large eggs
- 1 teaspoon Vanilla extract
- 1/8 teaspoon Salt
- Topping (optional)

Instructions:
1. Preheat oven to 350 degrees F (175 degrees C).
2. In a large bowl, mash bananas; stir in flour, sugar, cream, eggs, vanilla, and salt until blended.
3. Pour mixture into an ungreased 8x8 inch baking dish. Bake for 40 to 45 minutes. (Center will be slightly soft.)
4. Cool and serve with optional topping of your choice.

Nutrition Information:
Calories: 382 kcal, Protein: 4.4 g, Carbohydrates: 57 g, Fat: 14 g, Sodium: 86 mg.

32. Eggnog Custard

Eggnog Custard is a delicious, creamy, and indulgent dessert that's perfect for a festive treat. Serving 6-8 people, it takes 10 minutes of | Preparation Time and 40 minutes of cooking time.

Ingredients:
- 6 eggs
- 2 1/2 cups of whole milk
- 3/4 cup of white sugar
- 1 teaspoon of vanilla extract
- 1/4 teaspoon of ground nutmeg
- Pinch of salt

Instructions:
1. Preheat your oven to 350F (175° C).

2. In a medium bowl, whisk together the eggs, milk, sugar, vanilla extract, nutmeg, and salt until the ingredients are well blended.
3. Pour the mixture into a 9-inch round baking pan or a 9x13-inch baking dish.
4. Place the pan into a shallow water bath and bake for 40 minutes, or until the custard has set.
5. Serve warm and dust with a bit of ground nutmeg, if desired.

Nutrition Information:
Serving Size: 1/6 of the recipe
Calories: 225
Total Fat: 7.3 g
Saturated Fat: 3.7 g
Cholesterol: 131 mg
Sodium: 123 mg
Carbohydrates: 28.7 g
Sugar: 28.4 g
Protein: 8.2 g

33. Dulce De Leche Custard

Dulce de leche custard is a classic Latin American dessert that blends sweet and creamy flavors. This delightful treat is made with a simple mixture of sweetened condensed milk, flan, and dulce de leche for a delicious combination of indulgence and comfort.

Serving: 6 | Preparation Time: 25 minutes | Ready Time: 3 hours

Ingredients:
-14 ounces of sweetened condensed milk
4 eggs
-1/4 cup of dulce de leche
-1 tablespoon of vanilla
-2 cups of whole milk
-3/4 cup of granulated sugar
-1/4 teaspoon of salt

Instructions:
1. Preheat your oven to 350 degrees.
2. In a medium bowl, whisk together the sweetened condensed milk, eggs, dulce de leche, and vanilla.
3. In a large saucepan, heat the milk, sugar, and salt over medium-low heat, stirring constantly until the sugar dissolves.
4. Gradually add the milk mixture to the egg mixture, stirring constantly.
5. Grease a 9-inch baking dish and pour the custard mixture into it.
6. Place the baking dish into a large rimmed baking sheet and carefully fill the baking sheet with hot water, making sure the dish is not submerged.
7. Bake for 50 to 55 minutes, or until a knife inserted in the center comes out clean.
8. Remove from the oven and let cool for about an hour. Refrigerate for at least 2 hours before serving.

Nutrition Information:
Calories: 291, Total fat: 8.7g, Saturated fat: 4.3g, Cholesterol: 115mg, Sodium: 176mg, Carbohydrates: 41.1g, Protein: 9.6g

34. Coconut Cream Custard

Coconut Cream Custard is an indulgent yet simple dessert to put together - creamy and packed with flavor! This custard is sure to impress any dinner guest.

Serving: 8 | Preparation Time: 15 minutes | Ready Time: 1-2 hours

Ingredients:
- 2 cups unsweetened coconut cream
- 1/2 cup granulated sugar
- 1/2 teaspoon salt
- 2 eggs
- 2 tablespoons cornstarch
- 1 teaspoon vanilla extract

Instructions:
1. Preheat oven to 350°F.

2. In a large bowl, whisk together coconut cream, sugar, salt, eggs, and cornstarch.
3. Mix in the vanilla.
4. Grease an 8-inch baking dish and pour in the mixture.
5. Bake for 40 minutes, until the custard is golden and set.
6. Let cool for 15 minutes before serving.

Nutrition Information:
Serving size: 1/8 of custard
Calories: 341, Fat: 18g, Saturated Fat: 14.7g, Carbohydrates: 39.2g, Sugar: 28.6g, Sodium: 173.9mg, Protein: 4.7g.

35. Butterscotch Custard

Butterscotch Custard is a rich, creamy custard dessert made with brown sugar, butter and eggs. It is smooth, creamy and absolutely delicious.

Serving: 4-6 | Preparation Time: 10 minutes | Ready Time: 3 hours

Ingredients:
• 2 cups heavy cream
• 1/2 cup firmly packed brown sugar
• 2 tablespoons butter
• 4 large egg yolks
• 1/8 teaspoon ground nutmeg
• Dash of salt

Instructions:
1. Preheat oven to 300 degrees.
2. In medium saucepan, over medium heat, combine cream and bourbon; mix in other ingredients and stir until smooth.
3. Pour mixture into a double boiler and heat until mixture thickens, stirring occasionally.
4. Pour liquid into 4-6 small heat-resistant dishes and bake 30 minutes or until a knife inserted halfway into the center comes out clean.
5. Allow custards to cool before serving.

Nutrition Information (per serving):
Calories: 361, Fat: 26 g, Cholesterol: 208 mg, Sodium: 65 mg,
Carbohydrates: 21 g, Protein: 8 g

36. Spiced Apple Custard

Spice up your custard game with this delicious Spiced Apple Custard!
The delightful combination of apples and spices makes a creamy and
flavorful custard.

Serving: 6 | Preparation Time: 15 minutes | Ready Time: 1 hour

Ingredients:
• 4 cups peeled, chopped apples
• 2 tablespoons of butter
• 1 cup of sugar
• 3 eggs
• 4 cups of heavy cream
• 2 teaspoons nutmeg
• 2 teaspoons ground cinnamon
• 2 teaspoons ground ginger

Instructions:
1. Preheat the oven to 350F.
2. In a medium saucepan, melt the butter over low heat. Add the apples
and sugar and cook for about 5 minutes, stirring occasionally. Remove
from the heat.
3. In a large bowl, whisk the eggs until light and fluffy. Gradually whisk
in the cream and the apple mixture.
4. Add the nutmeg, cinnamon, and ginger and whisk to combine. Pour
the mixture into a greased 9x13 inch baking dish.
5. Bake for 45 minutes, or until the custard is set and golden brown. Let
cool before serving.

Nutrition Information:
Serving Size: 1/6 of recipe
Calories: 270 kcal

Total Fat: 17 g
Carbohydrates: 27 g
Protein: 4 g
Sodium: 35 mg
Cholesterol: 73 mg

37. White Chocolate Custard

White Chocolate Custard is a delicious, creamy dessert made with white chocolate and eggs that create a velvety custard that is sure to tantalize your taste buds!

Serving – 8, | Preparation Time – 20 minutes, Ready in – 120 minutes.

Ingredients:
• 7 oz white chocolate
• 4 egg yolks
• 1/2 cup heavy cream
• 1/2 cup of milk
• 2 tablespoons of granulated sugar
• Pinch of salt

Instructions:
1. Preheat oven to 350F/175°C.
2. Place the white chocolate in a heatproof bowl, and melt it in a microwave for 1 minute or until melted.
3. In a separate bowl, whisk together egg yolks, cream, milk, sugar and salt until combined.
4. Slowly add the melted white chocolate and whisk until mixture is well combined.
5. Pour the custard mixture into ramekins and place them in a water bath.
6. Bake in preheated oven for 35-45 minutes or until the surface of the custard becomes slightly puffy and golden.
7. Remove from oven and let cool for 30 minutes before serving.

Nutrition Information: Calories: 263, Fat: 15g, Saturated Fat: 9g, Cholesterol: 114mg, Sodium: 57mg, Potassium: 101mg, Carbohydrates: 25g, Fiber: 1g, Sugar: 17g, Protein: 4g

38. Pecan Pie Custard

Pecan Pie Custard is a delicious and comforting dessert, with a nutty and sweet flavor that is sure to please any occasion.

Serving: 8 | Preparation Time: 15 minutes | Ready Time: 1 hour

Ingredients:
- 9" unbaked pie crust
- 2 1/2 cups milk
- 1/2 cup light corn syrup
- 1/4 cup brown sugar
- 2 eggs
- 2 tablespoons melted butter
- 1 teaspoon vanilla extract
- 2/3 cup chopped pecans

Instructions:
1. Preheat oven to 325F.
2. In a medium mixing bowl, whisk together the milk, corn syrup, brown sugar, eggs, melted butter and vanilla extract until combined.
3. Spread the pecans in the pie crust, and pour the custard mixture over the top.
4. Place the pie on a baking sheet and bake in preheated oven for 30 to 35 minutes, or until center is set.
5. Allow pie to cool completely before serving.

Nutrition Information: Per Serving - 228 calories, 10 g fat, 4 g saturated fat, 30 mg cholesterol, 131 mg sodium, 33 g carbohydrate, 1g fiber, 5 g protein.

39. Cherry Cordial Custard

Cherry Cordial Custard is an indulgent, chocolatey and creamy dessert that will please any sweet tooth. It features a delectable custard base made with enriched chocolate and cream, mixed with pieces of cherry-filled cordials, and topped with more cherry pieces and chocolate drizzle.

Serving: 6-8 | Preparation Time: 20 minutes | Ready Time: 1 hour 30 minutes

Ingredients:
- 3 cups of heavy cream
- 2 cups of semi-sweet chocolate chips
- 1/4 cup granulated sugar
- 1 teaspoon of vanilla extract
- 1/4 teaspoon of salt
- 6 large Egg yolks
- 12 cherry cordials, chopped
- 1/4 cup of chocolate shavings
- 6-8 maraschino cherries, quartered

Instructions:
1. Preheat the oven to 350 degrees Fahrenheit.
2. In a medium saucepan over medium heat, combine the heavy cream, chocolate chips, sugar, vanilla extract, and salt. Stir continuously until the mixture reaches a light simmer.
3. In a separate bowl, whisk the egg yolks until light and fluffy. Slowly add the hot cream mixture to the bowl with the egg yolks and whisk until well combined.
4. Grease a 9-inch cake pan with butter and line the bottom with parchment paper. Pour the custard batter into the pan and top with chopped cherry cordials.
5. Bake in the preheated oven for 30-35 minutes, or until the bottom of the custard is golden brown.
6. Let the custard cool completely before topping with chocolate shavings and cherry quarters.

Nutrition Information: Each serving of Cherry Cordial Custard contains approximately 415 calories, 34g of fat, 18g of carbohydrates, 6g of protein, and 210mg of sodium.

40. Panna Cotta Custard

Panna Cotta Custard is an Italian-inspired dessert with a creamy, pudding-like texture. It is a delicious and simple way to enjoy a classic custard-style dessert.

Serving: 4 | Preparation Time: 10 minutes | Ready Time: 4 hours

Ingredients:
- 1/2 cup white sugar
- 1 envelope unflavored gelatin
- 2 cups heavy cream
- 1/2 cup whole milk
- 2 teaspoons vanilla extract
- pinch of salt

Instructions:
1. In a medium saucepan, whisk together the sugar, gelatin, cream, and milk.
2. Heat the mixture over medium heat, stirring until the sugar and gelatin dissolve and the mixture starts to bubble.
3. Remove the pan from the heat and stir in the vanilla and a pinch of salt.
4. Pour the mixture into 4 individual ramekins or dessert dishes, and transfer to the refrigerator.
5. Chill for at least 4 hours, or until the custard has set.

Nutrition Information (per serving):
Calories: 417 kcal, Carbohydrates: 25 g, Protein: 4 g, Fat: 33 g, Saturated Fat: 21 g, Cholesterol: 119 mg, Sodium: 88 mg, Potassium: 140 mg, Sugar: 23 g, Vitamin A: 1113 IU, Vitamin C: 1 mg, Calcium: 130 mg.

41. Huckleberry Custard

Try this delicious Huckleberry Custard for a sweet and creamy pudding-like treat. A summer classic, it's the perfect way to top off any get-together.

Serving: 6-8 | Preparation Time: 15 minutes | Ready Time: 30 minutes

Ingredients:
- 2 cups of huckleberries (fresh or frozen)
- 2 cups of heavy cream
- 2 whole eggs
- 1/3 cup of white sugar
- 2 teaspoons of vanilla extract

Instruction:
1. Preheat the oven to 350F and grease an 8-inch baking dish.
2. Boil the huckleberries and mash until smooth.
3. In a separate bowl, whisk together the cream, eggs, sugar and vanilla extract.
4. Pour the cream mixture and mashed huckleberries into the baking dish.
5. Bake for 30 minutes or until a knife inserted into the custard comes out clean.
6. Allow to cool completely before serving.

Nutrition Information:
Nutrition per serving:calories 164; fat 12.4g; carbohydrates 12.6g; protein 3.1g; cholesterol 62mg; sodium 32mg

42. White Chocolate Macadamia Nut Custard

White Chocolate Macadamia Nut Custard is a delightful, creamy dessert that combines the nutty goodness of macadamia nuts with sweet white chocolate and a smooth custard - a delicious combination that everyone can enjoy! This comforting dessert is sure to impress any crowd. Serving 4-6 people, this dish is great for gatherings with family and friends.

Serving: 4-6 | Preparation Time: 40 minutes | Ready Time: 2 hours

Ingredients:
- 3 1/4 cups heavy cream
- 4 large egg yolks
- 1/4 cup white sugar

- 2 thirds cup white chocolate chips
- 3/4 cup chopped macadamia nuts
- 1/2 teaspoon of vanilla extract

Instructions:
1. Heat the cream in a medium saucepan over medium heat until just simmering.
2. In a medium bowl, whisk together egg yolks, white sugar, and vanilla extract.
3. Pour the heated cream into the egg mixture while stirring continuously.
4. Pour the mixture back into the saucepan and heat, stirring constantly, until mixture thickens and coats the back of a spoon, around 5 minutes.
5. Place the white chocolate chips and chopped macadamia nuts in the bottom of 4-6 ramekins.
6. Pour the custard over the white chocolate chips and macadamia nuts until almost level with the top of the ramekins.
7. Place the ramekins in a roasting pan and fill the roasting pan with boiling water until it comes halfway up the sides of the ramekins.
8. Bake at 350F for 30 minutes or until the custard sets.
9. Remove the ramekins from the water and allow to cool before serving.

Nutrition Information: (per serving)
Calories: 604
Total Fat: 53g
Saturated Fat: 32g
Cholesterol: 205mg
Sodium: 92mg
Carbohydrates: 24g
Sugar: 20g
Protein: 7.2g

43. Tiramisu Custard

This Tiramisu Custard is the perfect crowd-pleaser with a creamy and delicious combination of espresso-soaked ladyfingers, ricotta cheese, and chocolate chips. It is the ideal dessert for any occasion!

Serving: 8 | Preparation Time: 25 minutes | Ready Time: 3 hours

Ingredients:
- 3 large eggs
- 3/4 cup sugar
- 2 cups ricotta cheese
- 1 cup heavy cream
- 1/4 teaspoon of salt
- 20 ladyfingers
- 1/2 cup strong espresso
- 1/4 cup semi-sweet chocolate chips
- 1/4 cup confectioners' sugar

Instructions:
1. Preheat oven to 350 degrees F (175 degrees C).
2. In a large bowl, beat eggs and sugar with an electric mixer until light and fluffy. Fold in ricotta cheese, cream, and salt.
3. Dip ladyfingers into espresso and place along the bottom of an 8-inch square baking dish. Spread half of the cheese mixture over ladyfingers. Sprinkle with half of the chocolate chips.
4. Bake in preheated oven for 25 minutes. Remove and let cool.
5. Sprinkle remaining chocolate chips over custard. Refrigerate for at least 3 hours before serving.
6. Dust with confectioners' sugar before serving. Enjoy!

Nutrition Information:
- Calories: 353
- Total Fat: 23.2g
- Cholesterol: 122mg
- Sodium: 150mg
- Carbohydrates: 23.4g
- Protein: 8.9g

44. Chocolate Walnut Brownie Custard

Chocolate Walnut Brownie Custard is an indulgent dessert that is sure to please! With intense chocolate flavor, crunchy walnuts, and a creamy custard texture, this recipe will be a hit with your family and friends.

Serving: 8 | Preparation Time: 20 minutes | Ready Time: 1 hour

Ingredients:
- 2 eggs
- 1 1/2 cups of granulated sugar
- 3/4 cup of all-purpose flour
- 1/3 cup of cocoa powder
- 1/2 teaspoon of baking powder
- 1/4 teaspoon of salt
- 1/2 cup of melted butter
- 1 teaspoon of vanilla extract
- 1/2 cup of chopped walnuts
- 2 cups of milk
- 1/4 teaspoon of ground cinnamon
- 1/4 teaspoon of ground nutmeg

Instructions:
1. Preheat oven to 350F and grease an 8-inch baking pan.
2. In a medium bowl, whisk together eggs and sugar until light and creamy.
3. In a separate bowl, mix together the flour, cocoa powder, baking powder and salt.
4. Gradually combine the wet and the dry ingredients, stirring until just blended.
5. Stir in the melted butter and vanilla until combined.
6. Gently fold in the chopped walnuts and spread the batter into the greased pan.
7. Bake for 20 minutes, and let cool completely.
8. In a small saucepan, heat milk, cinnamon and nutmeg over medium heat until just below a boil.
9. Remove from heat and whisk in 1 cup of sugar.
10. Beat together the eggs, remaining 1/2 cup of sugar, and flour until well blended.
11. Whisk the egg mixture into the milk and cook over low heat.

12. Continue to whisk until custard thickens, approximately 5 minutes.
13. Pour custard over the cooled brownies, spreading it evenly with a spatula.
14. Refrigerate for 1 hour before serving.

Nutrition Information: Per serving (1/8 of recipe): 286 calories, 15.8 g fat, 32.6 g carbohydrates, 4.3 g protein, 143 mg cholesterol, 181 mg sodium.

45. Cheesecake Custard

Cheesecake Custard is a rich, decadent and savory dessert. It combines creamy custard with a classic cheesecake base and topping to make an indulgent, delicious treat perfect for parties and special occasions.

Servings: 8 | Preparation Time: 20 minutes | Ready Time: 1 hour 15 minutes

Ingredients:
- 10 graham cracker sheets
- 1/4 cup melted butter
- 2 packages of cream cheese, softened
- 3/4 cup sugar
- 2 eggs
- 1/2 teaspoon vanilla
- 2 tablespoons all-purpose flour
- 2 tablespoons lemon juice
- 1 1/2 cups custard

Instructions:
1. Preheat your oven to 350F (176°C).
2. Crush the graham crackers and mix with the melted butter. Press the mixture into the bottom and up the sides of a 9-inch springform pan.
3. In a mixing bowl, beat the cream cheese and sugar together until it's light and fluffy.
4. Beat in the eggs, one at a time, stirring constantly.

5. Add the vanilla, flour and lemon juice and beat until the mixture is smooth.

6. Pour the mixture into the pan, spreading it evenly.

7. Dollop the custard over the cream cheese mixture making a design with a spoon.

8. Bake for 40 minutes.

9. Remove from oven and let cool, then refrigerate for at least 1 hour before serving.

Nutrition Information:
Per serving:
Calories: 286 kcal
Carbohydrates: 23 g
Protein: 6 g
Fat: 19 g
Saturated fat: 10 g
Cholesterol: 81 mg
Sodium: 274 mg
Potassium: 176 mg
Fiber: 1 g
Sugar: 16 g
Vitamin A: 610 IU
Calcium: 150 mg
Iron: 1 mg

46. Salted Caramel Custard

Salted Caramel Custard is a rich and decadent dessert made using creamy custard and salted caramel with a crunchy topping. It is sure to impress your guests and make an unforgettable treat.

Serving: 8-10 | Preparation Time: 15 minutes | Ready Time: 1.5 hours

Ingredients:
- 2 cups heavy cream
- 1/2 cup sugar
- Pinch of salt
- 6 large egg yolks

- 2 teaspoons vanilla extract
- 2/3 cup salted caramel

Instructions:
1. Preheat oven to 325F.
2. In a large saucepan, whisk together the cream, sugar, and salt. Bring the mixture to a boil over medium heat.
3. In a medium bowl, whisk together the egg yolks until combined.
4. Once the cream mixture is boiling, slowly add it to the egg yolks, whisking continuously until combined.
5. Pour the custard into a 9x13 inch baking dish.
6. Place the dish in a large roasting pan. Put the roasting pan into the preheated oven, then fill the roasting pan with water until it reaches two-thirds of the way up the side of the baking dish.
7. Bake in the preheated oven for 45 minutes.
8. Allow the custard to cool completely before adding the salted caramel.
9. Spread the cooled custard with the salted caramel, then refrigerate the custard until set.

Nutrition Information:
Per 1 serving: Calories 450,
Fat 34g,
Saturated Fat 21g,
Cholesterol 279mg,
Sodium 102mg,
Carbohydrates 29g,
Fiber 0g,
Sugar 24g,
Protein 5g.

47. Sweet Potato Custard

This Sweet Potato Custard is a creamy, slightly sweet, and perfectly spiced custard made with simple ingredients and minimal effort.

Serving: 8, | Preparation Time 10 minutes, ready time 6 hours,

Ingredients:
- 2 1/2lbs sweet potato, peeled and cubed
- 1 1/2 cups evaporated milk
- 1/2 cup sugar
- 2 large eggs, lightly beaten
- 2 teaspoon pumpkin pie spice
- 1/4 teaspoon salt
- 1/4 cup butter
- 2 tablespoons heavy cream

Instructions:
1. Preheat oven to 350F and grease a 9-inch round baking dish.
2. In a large saucepan, bring sweet potatoes and 1/2 cup of water to a boil. Reduce the heat and simmer for about 15 minutes or until potatoes are tender.
3. In a blender or food processor, combine cooked potatoes and the remaining ingredients. Blend until smooth.
4. Pour mixture into the prepared baking dish.
5. Bake for 30 minutes or until the custard is set.
6. Serve warm or at room temperature. Enjoy!

Nutrition Information: Serving Size 1/8 of recipe
Calories 231, Total fat 11.8g, Cholesterol 67mg, Sodium 232mg, Total Carbohydrates 28.7g, Dietary Fiber 2.5g, Protein 5.5g.

48. Coconut Lime Custard

Coconut Lime Custard is a classic South Asian dessert made with coconut milk, sugar, lime juice and eggs. This creamy, smooth and sweet custard is heavenly on its own or served with fresh fruit and condiments.

Serving: 6-8 | Preparation Time: 15 minutes | Ready Time: 45 minutes

Ingredients:
- 3/4 cup sugar
- 7 tablespoons cornstarch
- 1 can (14 ounces) coconut milk
- 2 large eggs

- 2 tablespoons butter
- 1/4 cup lime juice

Instructions:
1. In a medium saucepan, combine the sugar, cornstarch, and coconut milk. Place over medium heat and stir until combined.
2. Beat the eggs in a separate bowl with a whisk. Add the eggs to the mixture in the saucepan, stirring constantly with a wooden spoon. Cook until the mixture thickens, about 6 to 8 minutes.
3. Add the butter and lime juice and cook for an additional 2 minutes, stirring continuously.
4. Place the custard into a bowl and chill for at least 30 minutes before serving.

Nutrition Information:
Calories: 135; Total Fat: 9 g; Saturated Fat: 7.3 g; Cholesterol: 40 mg; Sodium: 25 mg; Total Carbohydrates: 11.5 g; Dietary Fiber: 0.5 g; Sugars: 8.5 g; Protein: 2.2 g.

49. Chocolate Mint Custard

Chocolate Mint Custard is a deliciously creamy pudding that is a perfect after-dinner treat. Rich in flavor, this custard has just the right balance between the sweet chocolate with a hint of mint.

Serving: 6-8 | Preparation Time: 15 minutes | | Ready Time: 55 minutes

Ingredients:
- 2 1/2 cups whole milk
- 6 egg yolks
- 2/3 cup sugar
- 1/4 cup all-purpose flour
- 2 tablespoons cocoa powder
- 1/4 teaspoon salt
- 2 tablespoons unsalted butter
- 1 teaspoon peppermint extract
- 2 ounces semi-sweet mini chocolate chips

Instructions:
1. Preheat oven to 350F. Grease a 9-inch baking dish with butter and set aside.
2. In a medium bowl, whisk together the egg yolks and sugar until fully combined and slightly pale in color.
3. In a medium saucepan, combine the milk, flour, cocoa powder, and salt over medium heat. Bring the mixture to a simmer, whisking until the ingredients are fully combined.
4. Gradually add the hot milk mixture to the egg yolk mixture, whisking constantly until smooth and creamy.
5. Pour the custard into the pre-greased baking dish and sprinkle the mini chocolate chips over the top.
6. Bake in preheated oven for 40-45 minutes, or until a knife inserted in the center comes out clean.
7. Remove from oven and let cool. Serve chilled.

Nutrition Information: Per serving, this Chocolate Mint Custard contains approximately 297 calories, 18.4g fat, 7.3g saturated fat and 12.4g protein.

50. Orange Cranberry Custard

Orange Cranberry Custard is an delicious dessert that combines sweet oranges and tart cranberries to make a delectable custard.

Serving: 8 to 10 | Preparation Time: 15 minutes | Ready Time: 20 minutes

Ingredients:
- 2 cups orange juice
- 2 cups cranberries
- 4 eggs
- 1/2 cup white sugar
- 1 teaspoon vanilla extract

Instructions:
1. Preheat oven to 350F. Grease a 9-inch round baking dish with butter.

2. In a medium saucepan, heat the orange juice and cranberries until simmering. Reduce heat and let cool for 5 minutes.
3. In a medium bowl, whisk eggs until frothy. Gradually add sugar and whisk until the sugar has dissolved.
4. Slowly stir in cooled orange juice and cranberry mixture.
5. Stir in vanilla extract.
6. Pour into prepared baking dish and bake in preheated oven for 15-20 minutes, or until a cake tester inserted into the center of the custard comes out clean.

Nutrition Information:
Per Serving:
157 calories, 4.2g fat, 28.2g carbohydrates, 3.2g protein

51. Mexican Chocolate Custard

This deliciously creamy Mexican Chocolate Custard combines traditional Mexican spices with sweet and creamy custard for a flavourful and indulgent dessert.

Serving: 4-6 | Preparation Time: 15 minutes | Ready Time: 75 minutes

Ingredients:
- 2 1/2 cups whole milk
- 1/2 teaspoon ground cinnamon
- 1/4 teaspoon ground red pepper
- 2 tablespoons cornstarch
- 1/4 cup plus 1/4 cup firmly packed light brown sugar
- 1/4 teaspoon ground nutmeg
- 6 egg yolks
- 4 ounces bittersweet chocolate, chopped
- 1/2 teaspoon pure vanilla extract
- 1/8 teaspoon salt

Instructions:
1. Preheat oven to 350F. In a medium saucepan over medium heat, combine milk, cinnamon, red pepper and cornstarch. Cook for about 10

minutes, stirring constantly, until the mixture thickens and begins to bubble around the edges.

2. In a medium bowl, whisk together brown sugar, nutmeg, egg yolks, chocolate, salt, and vanilla extract. Gradually whisk in the hot milk mixture.

3. Divide the custard among 4 to 6 oven-proof ramekins. Place into a larger baking dish and fill the dish with enough hot water to come halfway up the sides of the ramekins. Bake in oven until custards are set, about 45 to 50 minutes. Let cool completely before serving.

Nutrition Information:
Serving size: 1 cup
Calories: 238 kcal
Fat: 11.2g
Carbohydrates: 26.3g
Protein: 7.1g

52. Amaretto Sour Cherry Custard

This Amaretto Sour Cherry Custard is a creamy and flavorful dessert, perfect for any occasion. It combines the sweet flavors of amaretto and sour cherry and the smooth texture of rich custard for a delicious end to a meal.

Serving: Makes 4 servings | Preparation Time: 10 minutes | Ready Time: 40 minutes

Ingredients:
- 3/4 cup amaretto liquor
- 1/2 cup sugar
- 3 tablespoons cornstarch
- 1/4 teaspoon salt
- 2 1/2 cups whole milk
- 2 large eggs
- 1 teaspoon vanilla extract
- 2 cups sour cherries, pitted and halved

Instructions:

1. Preheat oven to 350F.

2. In a medium saucepan, combine the amaretto, sugar, cornstarch and salt, stirring until the cornstarch is dissolved.

3. Gradually stir in the milk, and cook over medium heat, stirring frequently, until the mixture comes to an almost boil and thickens.

4. Remove from heat and whisk in the eggs, vanilla extract and cherries.

6. Pour the mixture into four shallow oven safe dishes, and place into a baking dish.

7. Add 1/2 inch of hot water to the baking dish, and bake for 25-30 minutes, until the custard is set. Allow to cool before serving.

Nutrition Information (per serving): Calories: 320, Total Fat: 7g, Saturated Fat: 3.5g, Cholesterol: 106mg, Sodium: 240mg, Carbohydrates: 42g, Dietary Fibre: 1g, Protein: 10g.

53. Root Beer Float Custard

Root beer float custard is a creamy and flavorful dessert that combines the classic taste of root beer and delicious custard. This easy and fun dessert takes no time to prepare and can be enjoyed by all.

Serving: 4 | Preparation Time: 5 minutes | Ready Time: 2 hours

Ingredients:
- 2 cups whole milk
- 2 teaspoons pure vanilla extract
- 2 eggs
- 7 oz can of root beer
- 1/2 cup down sugar
- 1/2 teaspoon ground cinnamon
- Pinch of ground nutmeg
- 1/2 cup heavy cream
- Whipped cream for topping

Instructions:
1.Preheat the oven to 350° F (177° C).

2. In a medium bowl, whisk the milk, vanilla, eggs, root beer, sugar, cinnamon, and nutmeg until combined.
3. Pour the mixture into 4 ramekins and place them in a baking dish filled with water (enough to reach halfway up the sides).
4. Bake for 40-50 minutes, or until the custards are set.
5. Allow the custards to cool for about an hour before serving.
6. Top with heavy cream and a dollop of whipped cream to finish!

Nutrition Information:
Serving size: 1/4 root beer float custard; Calories: 265; Fat: 14.6g; Carbs: 28.9g; Protein: 6.3g.

54. Coffee Custard

Coffee Custard – a delicious rich, creamy and delicious dessert that is sure to please. A delicious combination of espresso and egg yolks is bound to win over the hearts of the lucky few who get to indulge in this treats.

Serving: 8 | Preparation Time: 15 minutes. | Ready Time: 30 minutes

Ingredients:
• 2 cups heavy cream
• 2 cups espresso
• 3/4 cup sugar
• 6 egg yolks
• 1 teaspoon vanilla extract

Instructions:
1. Preheat oven to 300F/150°C.
2. In a medium saucepan, heat the cream and espresso until it starts to boil.
3. In a medium bowl, whisk together the sugar and egg yolks until light and fluffy.
4. Gradually add the hot cream mixture to the egg and sugar mixture, whisking constantly.
5. Add in the vanilla extract.

6. Pour the custard into 8 ramekins or cups and place them in a 9-by-13 inch baking dish.

7. Pour boiling water into the baking dish, about halfway up the side of the cups, being careful not to get any water into the custard.

8. Bake in preheated oven for 30 minutes or until custard is set around the edges but slightly wobbly in the center.

9. Allow to cool before serving.

Nutrition Information:
• Calories: 333
• Fat: 19 g
• Cholesterol: 166 mg
• Sodium: 58 mg
• Carbohydrates: 32 g
• Fiber: 0 g
• Protein: 5 g

55. Spiced Pear Custard

This decadent and warm baked Spiced Pear Custard is an amazing choice for cold winter days or for a special brunch.

Serving: Serves 8 | Preparation Time: 10 minutes | Ready Time: 35 minutes

Ingredients:
- 6 pears, peeled, cored and cut into large cubes
- 2/3 cup sugar
- 2 tablespoons ground cinnamon
- 1 tablespoon ground nutmeg
- 2 cups heavy cream
- 2 teaspoons vanilla extract
- 6 large eggs, lightly beaten

Instructions:
1. Preheat oven to 350 degrees F. Grease an 8-inch square baking dish.
2. In a medium bowl, combine the pears, sugar, cinnamon, nutmeg and cream until the pears are thoroughly coated.

3. Pour the mixture into the prepared baking dish.

4. In a small bowl, mix together the vanilla extract and eggs. Gently pour the egg mixture over the pears.

5. Bake for 35 minutes or until lightly browned and a toothpick inserted into the center comes out clean.

Nutrition Information: Calories: 250; Total Fat: 16 g; Saturated Fat: 9 g; Cholesterol: 122 mg; Sodium: 74 mg; Carbohydrates: 24 g; Fiber: 3 g; Sugar: 19 g; Protein: 4 g.

56. Maple Bacon Custard

This Maple Bacon Custard is a divine combination of sweet and savory flavors and makes for a delicious breakfast item or tasty treat. Serves 8. | Preparation Time 10 minutes, Ready time 35 minutes.

Ingredients:
•4 large eggs
•1 cup maple syrup
•1/4 teaspoon ground nutmeg
•1/4 teaspoon ground cinnamon
•2 cups light cream or half-and-half
•1 teaspoon pure vanilla extract
•1/2 cup cooked and crumbled bacon

Instructions:
1. Preheat oven to 350F. Grease an 8-inch square baking pan with non-stick cooking spray.

2. In a large bowl, whisk together the eggs, maple syrup, nutmeg, and cinnamon.

3. Slowly pour in the cream while whisking. Add the vanilla extract and bacon.

4. Pour the mixture into the greased baking pan.

5. Bake the custard for 30-35 minutes, until the custard is set and golden brown.

6. Let cool before serving.

Nutrition Information: Serving Size: 1 (142g), Calories: 197, Fat: 11.7g, Saturated Fat: 6.2g, Cholesterol: 93mg, Sodium: 118mg, Carbohydrates: 17.4g, Fiber: 0.3g, Sugar: 17.2g, Protein: 4.8g.

57. Peanut Butter and Jelly Custard

This delicious and creamy Peanut Butter and Jelly Custard is the perfect dessert for any occasion. With the combination of salty and sweet, this yummy dish is sure to impress.

Servings: 4 | Preparation Time: 10 minutes | Ready Time: 45 minutes

Ingredients:
- 2 cups of heavy cream
- 1/2 cup of peanut butter
- 1/2 cup of strawberry jelly
- 4 egg yolks
- 1/2 cup of sugar
- 1 teaspoon of vanilla extract

Instructions:
1. Preheat oven to 350 degrees Fahrenheit.
2. In a medium sized bowl, whisk together the egg yolks and sugar until they are combined.
3. Heat the heavy cream in a medium saucepan over medium heat until it is just about to boil.
4. Slowly add the hot cream to the egg mixture, whisking constantly until all of the cream is added and the mixture is smooth and creamy.
5. Add the peanut butter, jelly and vanilla extract, stirring until the ingredients are combined.
6. Pour the custard into 4 individual ramekins or one large baking dish.
7. Bake in preheated oven for 35-40 minutes or until the custard is set.
8. Allow the custard to cool before serving.

Nutrition Information:
Serving Size: 1/4 of the custard
Calories: 422 calories

Fat: 26.3 g
Carbohydrates: 35.2 g
Protein: 10 g

58. Coconut Meringue Custard

Coconut Meringue Custard is a decadent yet light dessert made with sweetened condensed milk and freshly grated coconut. It is finished with creamy meringue for an extra special touch.

Serving: Makes 8 servings. | Preparation Time: 10 minutes | Ready Time: 2 hours

Ingredients:
- 1 can (14 ounces) sweetened condensed milk
- 2 eggs, lightly beaten
- 1 cup freshly grated coconut
- 1/3 cup sugar
- 1 teaspoon vanilla extract
- 3 egg whites
- 1/4 teaspoon cream of tartar

Instructions:
1. Preheat oven to 350 degrees F.
2. In a medium bowl, combine the condensed milk, eggs, coconut, sugar, and vanilla. Mix well.
3. Pour the mixture into an 8-inch baking dish.
4. In a separate bowl, beat the egg whites and cream of tartar on high speed until soft peaks form.
5. Add the sugar and continue to beat until stiff peaks form.
6. Spread the meringue on top of the custard in the baking dish.
7. Bake for 30 minutes, or until golden brown and custard is set.
8. Let cool before serving.

Nutrition Information:
Calories: 231; Fat: 10g; Saturated Fat: 6g; Carbohydrates: 30g; Sugar: 27g; Protein: 5g; Sodium: 81mg

59. Fig Custard

Fig Custard is a light and creamy dessert full of flavor. It can be served as a simple treat or with an extra layer of crunchy granola. This recipe is easy to make and can be enjoyed by everyone in the family.

Serving: 10 | Preparation Time: 40 minutes | Ready Time: 60 minutes

Ingredients:
- 2 cups figs, diced
- 4 eggs
- 2 cups whole milk
- 1/2 cup white sugar
- 2 teaspoons vanilla extract
- 1/4 teaspoon nutmeg
- 1/2 teaspoon ground cinnamon
- 1/2 cup granola (optional, for topping)

Instructions:
1. Preheat oven to 350F (177°C).
2. In a medium bowl, combine the diced figs, eggs, milk, sugar, vanilla extract, nutmeg, and cinnamon. Whisk together until combined.
3. Spray a 9-inch baking dish with non-stick cooking spray and pour the fig mixture into the dish.
4. Bake for 40 minutes, or until the custard is golden and lightly set.
5. Remove from oven and sprinkle with granola. Serve warm or cold.

Nutrition Information:
Serving Size: 1/10, Calories: 168, Carbs: 27g, Protein: 5.5g, Fat: 4.7, Cholesterol: 95.7mg, Sodium: 59.6mg, Potassium: 153.6mg, Fiber: 1.9g, Sugar: 18.2g.

60. Date Custard

Date Custard is a subtly sweet, creamy and flavorful dessert that combines dates with a traditional custard base. This dish is perfect for holiday meals and special occasions.

Serving: 6-8 | Preparation Time: 10 minutes | Ready Time: 1 hour

Ingredients:
-4 large eggs
-2 cups whole milk
-3/4 cup granulated sugar
-1/4 cup all-purpose flour
-1 teaspoon ground cinnamon
-1/2 teaspoon freshly grated nutmeg
-3/4 cup chopped pitted dates
-1 teaspoon vanilla extract
-1/2 teaspoon sea salt

Instructions:
1. Preheat oven 350F.
2. In a medium bowl, whisk together eggs and milk; set aside.
3. In a separate bowl, mix together sugar, flour, cinnamon, nutmeg, and salt; set aside.
4. Add the sugar mixture into the egg-milk mixture and whisk until combined.
5. Add the dates and vanilla extract, whisk until combined.
6. Grease a 9x9-inch baking dish.
7. Pour the custard into the prepared baking dish and bake for 40 minutes, until the custard is slightly golden and set in the center.
8. Remove from oven and let cool before serving.

Nutrition Information (per serving):
Calories: 187
Total Fat: 6 g
Saturated Fat: 3 g
Cholesterol: 82 mg
Sodium: 182 mg
Carbohydrates: 29 g
Fiber: 1 g
Sugar: 23 g
Protein: 6 g

61. Rhubarb Custard

Rhubarb Custard is a delicious and creamy dessert that is packed with flavour. The simple combination of rhubarb, custard and a few other ingredients creates a wonderful treat that the whole family can enjoy.

Servings: 3 | Preparation Time: 15 minutes | Ready Time: 40 minutes

Ingredients:
- 150g rhubarb, cut into 5cm pieces
- 160g caster sugar
- 2 tbsp cornflour
- 300ml double cream
- 200ml whole milk
- 2 eggs, beaten
- 1/2 tsp ground ginger
- 1/2 tsp ground cinnamon

Instructions:
1. Preheat your oven to 180°C/350F.
2. Grease a 20cm ovenproof dish with butter and scatter the rhubarb across the bottom.
3. In a large bowl, mix together the sugar, cornflour, cream, milk, eggs and spices until fully combined.
4. Carefully pour the custard mixture over the rhubarb in the ovenproof dish. Bake in the oven for 40 minutes.
5. Serve Rhubarb Custard with a dollop of cream, if desired.

Nutrition Information: Per Serving – Calories: 372, Fat: 21.2g, Carbohydrates: 40.9g, Protein: 5.3g

62. Fresh Apple Pie Custard

Fresh Apple Pie Custard is a delicious and easy to bake treat, perfect for a dessert. It is a creamy, caramely custard packed with sweet, juicy apples.

Serving: 8-10 | Preparation Time: 10 minutes | Ready Time: 40 minutes

Ingredients:
- 5 Apples
- 2 cups Heavy Cream
- 1/2 cup Sugar
- 1/2 teaspoon Vanilla Extract
- 1/4 teaspoon Salt
- 1/4 teaspoon Ground Cinnamon
- 1/4 teaspoon Ground Nutmeg
- Complentary store-bought or homemade pie crust

Instructions:
1. Preheat oven to 350F.
2. Peel and slice the apples. Place in a medium bowl.
3. In a separate bowl, whisk together cream, sugar, vanilla extract, salt, cinnamon and nutmeg.
4. Place pie crust into a 9-inch pie dish.
5. Arrange the apples in the pie crust.
6. Pour the cream mixture over the apples.
7. Cover with aluminum foil and bake for 30 minutes.
8. Remove foil and bake for 10-15 additional minutes, until the crust is golden brown and center is set.
9. Let cool for 15 minutes before serving.

Nutrition Information: Serving Size 1/10 of pie, Calories 250, Fat 10g, Carbs 37g, Fiber 2g, Protein 2g, Sugar 18g

63. Salted Honey Custard

Salted Honey Custard is a delicious and decadent dessert that combines sweet honey and creamy custard with a hint of salt. The result is a comforting, creamy treat that is sure to delight everyone at your dinner table!

Serving: 4-6 people | Preparation Time: 20 minutes | Ready Time: 3 hours

Ingredients:
- 2 cups of heavy cream

- 2/3 cup of granulated sugar
- 4 large eggs
- 1/4 cup of honey
- 1 teaspoon of salt
- 1 teaspoon of vanilla extract

Instructions:
1. Preheat your oven to 350F.
2. In a large bowl, whisk together the cream, sugar, eggs, honey, salt and vanilla extract until combined.
3. Pour the mixture into a lightly greased 9-inch baking pan.
4. Bake the custard for 40 minutes, or until the center is set and the top is golden brown.
5. Allow the custard to cool completely before serving.

Nutrition Information:
Per serving: 402 kcal, 19.3 g fat, 43.3 g carbohydrates, 5.7 g protein.

64. Spanakopita Custard

Spanakopita Custard is an indulgent and flavorful Greek dish of creamy custard filled with spinach and feta cheese, topped with a tasty phyllo crust. This comforting and delicious treat is sure to be a household favorite!

Serving: 6-8 | Preparation Time: 45 minutes | Ready Time: 1 hour

Ingredients:
- 2 tablespoons butter
- 2 tablespoons all-purpose flour
- 2 cups whole milk
- 1/2 cup grated Parmesan cheese
- 2 tablespoons minced garlic
- 1 cup chopped spinach
- 1 cup chopped onions
- 1 cup crumbled feta cheese
- 1/2 teaspoon hot pepper flakes
- 1/2 teaspoon dried oregano

- 1/8 teaspoon nutmeg
- Salt and pepper to taste
- 2 sheets store-bought phyllo dough, thawed
- 2 tablespoons butter, melted

Instructions:
1. Preheat oven to 375F.
2. In a medium saucepan, melt butter over medium heat.
3. Add flour and stir until smooth.
4. Gradually add the milk and stir until thickened.
5. Add the Parmesan cheese, garlic, spinach, onions, feta cheese, hot pepper flakes, oregano, nutmeg, salt, and pepper. Stir until combined.
6. Grease an oven-proof baking dish with butter.
7. Layer the phyllo dough on the bottom and sides of the baking dish, leaving some to use as a top layer.
8. Pour the custard mixture into the baking dish.
9. Place the remaining phyllo dough on top and brush it with melted butter.
10. Bake for 30-35 minutes, until golden brown and bubbling.

Nutrition Information:
Calories: 125, Total Fat: 7g, Saturated Fat: 4g, Cholesterol: 19mg, Sodium: 227mg, Carbohydrates: 8g, Protein: 5g

65. Lavender Honey Custard

A simple yet sweet and fragrant dessert, Lavender Honey Custard is silky smooth custard flavored with honey, vanilla and fragrant lavender.

Serving: 8 | Preparation Time: 20 minutes | Ready Time: 2 hours

Ingredients:
2 1/2 cups heavy cream
2 tablespoons dried lavender
1/2 cup honey
2 teaspoons vanilla
4 eggs
1/2 teaspoon salt

Instructions:
1. Preheat oven to 325 degrees F.
2. In a small saucepan over medium heat, add cream and lavender. Simmer for about 10 minutes until infused with the lavender flavor. Strain the lavender and let the cream cool for 5 minutes.
3. In a medium bowl, whisk together the honey, vanilla, eggs, and salt.
4. Add the cooled cream to the egg mixture and whisk together until fully combined.
5. Grease an 8-inch baking dish and pour the custard mixture into it.
6. Place the baking dish in an ovenproof pan and add enough hot water to the pan to come halfway up the dish.
7. Bake at 325 degrees F for 40-45 minutes, or until the custard is just set.
8. Let the custard cool to room temperature before serving.

Nutrition Information (per serving):
Calories: 281, Fat: 22g, Carbs: 15g, Protein: 6g

66. Cinnamon Roll Custard

Cinnamon Roll Custard is a sweet and savory dish that combines the delicious flavors of cinnamon rolls with creamy custard. Enjoy this decadent dish as a treat for breakfast, dessert, or even a snack.

Serving: 8 | Preparation Time: 10 minutes | Ready Time: 40 minutes

Ingredients:
-1/4 cup butter
-1 package cinnamon rolls with icing
-3 eggs
-1/4 cup granulated sugar
-1/4 teaspoon ground cinnamon
-1 teaspoon vanilla extract
-3 cups milk
-1 teaspoon kosher salt

Instructions:
1. Preheat oven to 350 degrees.

2. In a large skillet, melt butter over medium-high heat. Squeeze the cinnamon rolls onto the skillet and cook for 3-5 minutes or until lightly golden.
3. Remove from heat and let cool. Once cooled, break into small pieces and place in a 9x13 inch baking dish.
4. In a medium bowl, whisk together eggs, sugar, cinnamon, vanilla, and milk. Pour the mixture over the cinnamon roll pieces.
5. Sprinkle the kosher salt on top.
6. Bake for 30-35 minutes or until the custard is cooked through.
7. Serve warm with the cinnamon roll icing.

Nutrition Information:
Calories: 141 kcal, Carbohydrates: 15 g, Protein: 5 g, Fat: 8 g, Saturated Fat 5 g, Cholesterol: 45 mg, Sodium: 315 mg, Potassium: 143 mg, Fiber: 1 g, Sugar: 10 g, Vitamin A: 311 IU, Calcium: 96 mg, Iron: 0.4 mg

67. Toffee Custard

Toffee Custard is a delectably indulgent dessert that is the perfect combination of creamy and crunchy. A simple and delicious custard made with crunchy toffee pieces and a rich custard custard, this exquisite dish is an ideal way to end any meal.

Serving: 6 | Preparation Time: 15 minutes | Ready Time: 45 minutes

Ingredients:
-3-4 tablespoons toffee pieces
-3 tablespoons cornstarch
-3 eggs
-1/4 cup caster sugar
-2 cups milk
-2 tablespoons butter
-2 teaspoons vanilla extract

Instructions:
1. Preheat oven to 350F (175°C). Grease and flour a round 9-inch baking dish.

2. In a medium bowl, mix together the toffee pieces and cornstarch.

3. In a separate bowl, whisk together the eggs and sugar until light and fluffy. Slowly add in the milk, whisking until fully combined.

4. Slowly add the egg mixture and toffee pieces to the baking dish. Add the butter and vanilla extract. Mix until fully combined.

5. Bake in preheated oven for 40 minutes, or until the custard is set and the top is lightly golden.

Nutrition Information:
Serving size: 1/6 of the recipe
Calories: 288
Total Fat: 12g
Total Carbohydrates: 40g
Protein: 5g
Sodium: 113mg
Cholesterol: 95mg

68. Chai Spice Custard

Chai Spice Custard is a divinely creamy and flavorful dessert that is bursting with tantalizing spices. With a simple and straightforward 4-step process, you can have this delicious treat ready in no time.

Serving: 8 | Preparation Time: 20 minutes | Ready in: 40 minutes

Ingredients:
• 1/4 cup granulated sugar
• 2 tablespoons cornstarch
• 1/4 teaspoon ground cardamom
• 1/4 teaspoon ground cinnamon
• 1/4 teaspoon ground ginger
• Pinch of nutmeg
• 2 cups whole milk
• 2 egg yolks
• 2 tablespoons unsalted butter
• 2 tablespoons dark rum

Instructions:
1. In a medium-sized mixing bowl, whisk together sugar, cornstarch, cardamom, cinnamon, ginger, and nutmeg until blended.
2. In a small saucepan over medium heat, bring milk to a gentle boil. Remove from heat.
3. Slowly whisk the warm milk into the sugar-spice mix until well blended.
4. Pour into a medium saucepan, and place it over medium-low heat. Whisk in egg yolks, butter, and rum. Cook while whisking constantly until custard is thick and creamy.
5. Transfer custard to a bowl and cover with plastic wrap, pressing it against the surface of the custard to prevent a skin from forming. Refrigerate for about 20 minutes before serving.

Nutrition Information: per 1/2 cup serving:
Calories: 190, Fat: 8.8g, Saturated Fat: 5.1g, Cholesterol: 81mg, Sodium: 43mg, Carbohydrates: 21g, Fiber: 0g, Protein: 4g

69. Gingersnap Custard

Gingersnap Custard:Experience rich, creamy custard with the signature flavor of gingersnaps in this comforting dessert.

Serving: 10 | Preparation Time: 25 minutes | Ready Time: 2 hours

Ingredients:
-2 1/2 cups whole milk
-1/2 cup granulated sugar
-1/4 teaspoon ground ginger
-1/4 teaspoon salt
-3 large eggs
-2 teaspoons vanilla extract
-3/4 cup gingersnaps, crushed

Instructions:
1. Preheat oven to 350 degrees F.
2. In a small saucepan, heat the milk, sugar, ginger, and salt over medium heat until the mixture is just beginning to boil.

3.In a medium bowl, whisk together the eggs and vanilla until combined.
4. Slowly add the hot milk mixture to the eggs, whisking constantly until fully combined.
5. Add the crushed gingersnaps to the custard mixture and stir until combined.
6. Pour the custard into a greased baking dish and bake for 40-45 minutes or until the custard is just set.
7. Allow the custard to cool to room temperature before serving.

Nutrition Information: Per serving (1/10) - Calories 211.5, Fat 10.1 g, Carbohydrates 22.9 g, Protein 5.4 g

70. Malted Milk Custard

Malted Milk Custard is an old-fashioned dessert with a rich, indulgent flavors. This comforting treat features a creamy, velvety texture and comforting warm flavors of malted milk and vanilla.

Serving: 8 servings | Preparation Time: 15 minutes | Ready Time: 40 minutes

Ingredients:
- 2 cups whole milk
- 3 tablespoons malted milk powder
- 3 tablespoons granulated sugar
- 3 large egg yolks
- 1 teaspoon pure vanilla extract
- Pinch of salt

Instruction:
1. Preheat the oven to 325 degrees F. Place 8 (6- or 8-ounce) ramekins or custard cups in a 9x13-inch baking dish.
2. In a medium saucepan over medium-high heat, heat the milk until it starts to steam. Whisk in the malted milk powder and sugar. Reduce heat to medium and continue whisking until the powder and sugar dissolve.
3. In a medium bowl, whisk the egg yolks until pale. Slowly pour the hot milk into the bowl, whisking constantly. Whisk in the vanilla and salt.

4. Pour the custard mixture into the prepared ramekins or custard cups. Fill the baking dish with enough warm tap water to reach halfway up the sides of the cups.
5. Bake for 30 to 35 minutes, or until the custards are just set in the center.
6. Carefully remove the custards from the water bath and let cool slightly. Serve warm or at room temperature.

Nutrition Information: 123 calories; 6g fat; 13g carbohydrates; 4g protein; 0g fiber; 81mg cholesterol; 63mg sodium.

71. Banana Cream Pie Custard

Banana Cream Pie Custard is an indulgent and creamy dessert with a sweet, banana-flavored custard. Serves 8. | Preparation Time: 20 minutes. | Ready Time: 3 hours.

Ingredients:
- 3/4 cup granulated sugar
- 3 tablespoons cornstarch
- 3 cups whole milk
- 4 large egg yolks
- 1 teaspoon vanilla extract
- 1/2 teaspoon salt
- 2 ripe bananas, mashed
- 1/4 cup cold, unsalted butter
- 9-inch unbaked pastry crust

Instructions:
1. Preheat oven to 350 degrees F.
2. In a medium saucepan, whisk the sugar and cornstarch together. Slowly whisk in the milk until everything is well combined, then add the egg yolks. Place the saucepan over low heat and whisk.
3. Bring the mixture to a simmer and continue to whisk for 3 minutes. Remove the pan from the heat and stir in the vanilla extract and salt.
4. Pour the mixture into the unbaked pastry crust and add in the mashed bananas. Dot the top of the custard with the cold butter.

5. Bake in the preheated oven for 40 minutes, or until the top is golden brown and the custard is set.
6. Cool completely on a wire rack before serving.

Nutrition Information:
Calories: 268kcal, Carbohydrates: 32g, Protein: 5g, Fat: 12g, Saturated Fat: 7g, Cholesterol: 103mg, Sodium: 152mg, Potassium: 171mg, Fiber: 1g, Sugar: 19g, Vitamin A: 510IU, Vitamin C: 3.2mg, Calcium: 107mg, Iron: 1.1mg

72. Red Velvet Custard

Red Velvet Custard is a luxurious and indulgent dessert consisting of a velvety layers of cream and ancient flavour made from cocoa and beetroot. Enjoy this unique combination that's sure to tantalise your taste buds.

Serving: 6-8 people | Preparation Time: 20 minutes | Ready Time: 2 hours (including chilling time)

Ingredients:
- 1 cup of heavy cream
- 4 tablespoons of butter
- 4 ounces of cream cheese
- 1 teaspoon of Vanilla
- 2 tablespoons of cocoa powder
- 3/4 cup of beetroot puree
- 1/3 cup of icing sugar
- 2 tablespoons of cornstarch
- 3 egg yolks
- 1/2 teaspoon of salt

Instructions:
1. Preheat oven to 350F (175°C).
2. In a medium saucepan, melt butter and cream cheese together over low heat. Stir until combined and smooth.
3. Add heavy cream, vanilla and cocoa powder. Stir until combined and smooth.

4. Whisk in beetroot, icing sugar, cornstarch and salt until combined.
5. In a separate bowl, whisk egg yolks until lightly beaten.
6. Slowly pour egg yolks into the cream mixture, stirring constantly until combined.
7. Pour the custard into a 9-inch (23 cm) round cake pan and bake in preheated oven for 30 minutes.
8. Allow the custard to cool completely before serving.

Nutrition Information:
Calories – 240 kcal, Carbohydrates – 17 g, Fat – 16 g, Protein – 5 g, Sodium – 510 mg, Sugars – 10 g.

73. Key Lime Pie Custard

Key Lime Pie Custard is a zesty and refreshing dessert. It is a combination of sweet and tangy flavors, with an indulgent custard-like texture. Serving 8 people, this dessert can be prepared in 15 minutes and will be ready in 1 hour.

Ingredients:
- 2 cans (14 oz. each) sweetened condensed milk
- 3/4 cup lime juice
- 4 egg yolks
- 1 teaspoon lime zest
- 1 9-inch baked pie crust
- Whipped cream (optional)

Instructions:
1. Preheat oven to 350F
2. In a bowl, whisk together condensed milk, lime juice, egg yolks, and lime zest.
3. Pour the mixture into pre-baked pie crust.
4. Bake for 35 minutes or until the center of the pie is set.
5. Cool completely before serving.
6. Garnish with whipped cream if desired.

Nutrition Information: Per Serving (1/8th of pie): 268 calories, 12.6 g fat, 31.8 g carbohydrates, 4.6 g protein, 86.7 mg cholesterol, 93.3 mg sodium.

74. Chocolate Raspberry Custard

This delectable Chocolate Raspberry Custard is the perfect combination of tart and sweet. Packed with delicious flavor, it's sure to become a favorite!

Serving: 8 | Preparation Time: 10 minutes | Ready Time: 50 minutes

Ingredients:
- 8 ounces bittersweet chocolate, chopped
- 3 tablespoons unsalted butter
- 1 cup heavy cream
- 1 cup whole milk
- 1/2 cup granulated sugar
- 1/4 cup cornstarch
- 1 teaspoon vanilla extract
- 1/4 teaspoon salt
- 2 large eggs
- 1/4 cup raspberry preserves

Instructions:
1. Preheat oven to 325F.
2. In a medium heat-proof bowl, melt chocolate and butter over a double boiler, stirring until smooth.
3. In a medium saucepan, whisk together cream, milk, sugar, cornstarch, vanilla, and salt. Bring to a low boil, stirring occasionally.
4. Gradually whisk the hot cream mixture into the melted chocolate, stirring constantly.
5. In a small bowl, whisk together the eggs. Gradually whisk the eggs into the chocolate mixture, stirring constantly.
6. Pour the custard into eight 4-ounce ramekins. Place ramekins in a deep baking dish.

7. Place the baking dish in the preheated oven and pour in hot water until it reaches halfway up the sides of the ramekins.
8. Bake for 40-45 minutes, or until the custards are set.
9. Remove from oven, cool for 10 minutes.
10. Drizzle with raspberry preserves before serving.

Nutrition Information:
Serving Size: 1 custard
Calories: 285
Total Fat: 20.1g
Saturated Fat: 12.3g
Trans Fat: 0.0g
Sodium: 183mg
Carbohydrates: 18.4g
Fiber: 1.2g
Sugar: 11.1g
Protein:5.5g

75. Banana Split Custard

Banana Split Custard is a delicious and sweet dessert that combines creamy custard with crunchy bananas, chocolate chips, and walnuts into one dish.

Serving: 4-6 people, | Preparation Time is 15 minutes, ready in 30 minutes.

Ingredients:
- 2 1/2 cups of whole milk
- 3/4 cup granulated sugar
- 1 teaspoon plain gelatin
- 3 egg yolks
- 1 teaspoon of vanilla extract
- 2 ripe bananas, sliced
- 1/3 cup walnuts, chopped
- 1/2 cup semi-sweet chocolate chips

Instructions:
1. In a medium saucepan, combine the milk and 1/4 cup of the sugar over low heat. Stir until the sugar is dissolved.
2. In a small bowl, mix together the gelatin and the remaining sugar until blended. Stir into the milk until dissolved.
3. In a large bowl, whisk together the egg yolks and vanilla until blended. Gradually add the hot milk, whisking constantly to prevent the eggs from curdling.
4. Return the mixture to the saucepan. Cook over low heat, stirring constantly, until the custard thickens and coats the back of a spoon (170 degrees F).
5. Pour the custard into a bowl and let cool.
6. Place the cooled custard in the bottom of a 9-inch pie plate. Arrange the sliced bananas over the custard and sprinkle with the walnuts and chocolate chips.
7. Refrigerate until set, at least 2 hours.

Nutrition Information:
Calories: 232, Fat: 11.2g, Cholesterol: 101.3mg, Sodium: 25.6mg, Carbohydrates: 29.4g, Protein: 5.4g

76. Vanilla Bean Cheesecake Custard

This creamy, delicious Vanilla Bean Cheesecake Custard is a delicious indulgence perfect for any special occasion.

Serving: Makes 8 servings | Preparation Time: 15 minutes | Ready Time: 4-6 hours

Ingredients:
- 2 packages (8 ounces each) of cream cheese, softened
- 1/2 cup plus 1/3 cup granulated sugar
- 2 tablespoons unsalted butter, melted
- 2 teaspoons pure vanilla extract
- 1 vanilla bean, scraped
- 2 eggs
- 2/3 cup heavy cream
- 2/3 cup sour cream

Instructions:
1. Preheat oven to 350 degrees F (175 degrees C), line an 8-inch springform pan with parchment paper.
2. In the bowl of an electric mixer, combine the cream cheese and 1/2 cup of sugar and mix until smooth.
3. Add in the butter and mix until combined.
4. Add in vanilla extract, scraped vanilla bean and mix until combined.
5. Add eggs, one at a time, mixing until just blended.
6. Add in heavy cream, sour cream and remaining 1/3 cup of sugar and mix until blended.
7. Pour batter into the prepared springform pan.
8. Bake for 1 hour and 15 minutes, or until set and golden brown on top.
9. Allow to cool completely before serving.

Nutrition Information: Per Serving: 332 calories; 23.1 g fat; 5.9 g carbohydrates; 9.1 g protein; 71 mg cholesterol; 248 mg sodium.

77. Butter Pecan Custard

Butter Pecan Custard is a deliciously sweet, creamy custard topped with crunchy toasted pecans. It's simple to prepare, rich, and a comforting dessert for any season.

Serving: 8 | Preparation Time: 20 minutes | Ready Time: 1 hour

Ingredients:
- 5 large egg yolks
- 1 can (14 oz)sweetened condensed milk
- 2 cups half-and-half cream
- 3 tablespoons cornstarch
- 2 tablespoons butter or margarine, melted
- 2 teaspoons vanilla
- 1/4 teaspoon salt
- 2/3 cup finely chopped pecans, toasted

Instructions:
1. Preheat oven to 350F. Grease a 1 1/2-quart baking dish.
2. In a medium bowl, beat egg yolks; gradually beat in condensed milk.

3. In a small saucepan, combine half-and-half cream, cornstarch, butter, vanilla, and salt.
4. Cook over medium heat, stirring constantly, until mixture thickens and boils. Boil and stir 1 minute.
5. Gradually stir egg mixture into the cream mixture; blend until smooth. Pour into the prepared baking dish.
6. Sprinkle with the toasted pecans. Bake for 45 minutes, or until set. Cool.

Nutrition Information:
per serving:
Calories: 320
Total Fat: 15g
Saturated Fat: 8g
Cholesterol: 90mg
Sodium: 170mg
Carbohydrates: 36g
Fiber: 1g
Protein: 7g

78. Egg Custard

Egg Custard is a classic, creamy custard dessert that's easy to make and can be served either warm or cold, depending on your preference. It's a versatile recipe, perfect for breakfast, lunch, or dessert.

Serving: 4 | Preparation Time: 10 minutes | Ready Time: 1 hour

Ingredients:
• 4 eggs
• 1 cup sugar
• 4 cups milk
• 1 teaspoon vanilla

Instructions:
1. Preheat the oven to 350F (176°C).
2. In a large bowl, whisk together the eggs and sugar until completely smooth.

3. Slowly pour in the milk while stirring, then stir in the vanilla.
4. Grease four 6-ounce custard cups and divide the custard mixture among them.
5. Place the custard cups in a shallow baking dish and set the dish in the oven.
6. Pour enough hot water into the dish to come halfway up the custard cups.
7. Bake for 40 minutes or until the custard is set.
8. Let cool before serving.

Nutrition Information:
Calories: 205, Total fat: 8g, Cholesterol: 129mg, Sodium: 73mg, Total carbohydrate: 24g, Protein: 11g

79. Irish Cream Custard

Irish Cream Custard is a decadent dessert with a creamy texture and sweet flavor that can be enjoyed by everyone. It has a smooth, rich taste and a hint of Irish Cream liqueur that gives it an intoxicating flavor. The custard is incredibly easy to make, and it's sure to please even the pickiest of eaters!

Serving: 4 | Preparation Time: 10 minutes | Ready Time: 40 minutes

Ingredients:
• 2 cups heavy cream
• 3/4 cup sugar
• 6 egg yolks
• 1/4 cup Irish cream liqueur
• Pinch of salt

Instructions:
1. Preheat oven to 325F.
2. In a medium-sized saucepan, heat cream and sugar over medium heat, stirring constantly until the sugar has dissolved.
3. In a separate bowl, lightly beat the egg yolks.
4. Gradually add the eggs to the cream and sugar mixture and whisk to combine.

5. Add the Irish cream liqueur and salt, stirring to incorporate.
6. Pour the mixture into 6-8 ramekins, lightly greased with butter.
7. Place ramekins on a baking sheet and transfer to oven.
8. Bake for 25-30 minutes, or until custards are set and golden.
9. Remove from oven and let cool.
10. Serve chilled and garnish with a sprinkle of freshly grated nutmeg.

Nutrition Information:
• Calories: 311
• Total Fat: 23.4 g
• Saturated Fat: 13.7 g
• Cholesterol: 228 mg
• Sodium: 62 mg
• Total Carbohydrates: 18.1 g
• Dietary Fiber: 0.2 g
• Sugars: 17.7 g
• Protein: 4.1 g

80. Lemon Ginger Custard

This divine Lemon Ginger Custard is a silky, creamy and delightfully zesty dessert that bursts with flavour and is sure to tantalise your taste buds.

Serving: 8 | Preparation Time: 10 minutes | Ready Time: 2 hours

Ingredients:
- 2 cups of heavy cream
- 2/3 cup of sugar
- 2 teaspoons of freshly grated ginger
- 5 large egg yolks
- 2 tablespoons of fresh lemon juice
- pinch of salt

Instructions:
1. Whisk the heavy cream, sugar, and freshly grated ginger together in a medium saucepan over medium-high heat. Cook until the mixture is hot, stirring frequently.

2. Remove from heat and allow to cool for about 5 minutes.
3. Whisk the egg yolks and lemon juice together in a separate bowl.
4. Gradually add the cooled cream mixture to the egg yolk mixture while whisking.
5. Pour the custard mixture into 8 small ramekins or custard dishes.
6. Place in a large baking dish filled with 1 inch of hot water.
7. Bake at 350F (176°C) for 30-35 minutes until the custards are set.
8. Let cool before serving.

Nutrition Information:
Calories: 204, Fat: 11 g, Carbs: 23 g, Protein: 4 g.

81. Mocha Custard

This decadent Mocha Custard is the perfect way to satisfy a sweet tooth and get your coffee fix in one go. It's a rich and creamy custard made with espresso and cocoa powder and topped with a layer of buttery, golden crunch. Best served with some fresh raspberries or a dollop of whipped cream, this dessert is sure to please everyone at the dinner table.

Serving: 8-10 | Preparation Time: 15 minutes | Ready Time: 1-2 hours

Ingredients:
- 2 1/2 cups of low-fat milk
- 1/3 cup of espresso
- 3 egg yolks
- 1/3 cup of sugar
- 2 tablespoons of cocoa powder
- 1/2 teaspoon of vanilla extract
- 2 tablespoons of butter

Instructions:
1. Preheat the oven to 350F and lightly butter an 8-inch baking dish.
2. Heat the milk and espresso in a saucepan over medium heat.
3. In a separate bowl, whisk together the egg yolks, sugar, cocoa powder, and vanilla extract.
4. Slowly add the warm espresso mixture to the egg mixture, whisking constantly.

5. Transfer the mixture to the prepared baking dish.
6. Place the dish into the oven, and bake for 25-30 minutes.
7. Remove the custard from the oven and let cool.
8. Cut the butter into small cubes and sprinkle evenly over the custard.
9. Chill the custard before serving.

Nutrition Information:
Serving size: 1
Calories: 125
Total Fat: 4.2 grams
Total Carbohydrate: 15.2 grams
Protein: 4.6 grams

82. Avocado Custard

Introducing Avocado Custard - a pillowy, delicious pudding dessert that's as easy to make as it is to enjoy. With its creamy and light texture, this creamy custard is sure to make a mouthwatering treat for everyone!

Serving: 4 | Preparation Time: 10 minutes | Ready Time: 90 minutes

Ingredients:
- 2 avocados, mashed
- 2 cups whole milk
- 3/4 cup sugar
- 2 egg yolks
- 2 tablespoons all-purpose flour
- 1 teaspoon vanilla extract
- Pinch of salt

Instructions:
1. In a medium bowl, mash the avocados until smooth.
2. In a small saucepan, heat the milk and sugar over medium-high heat, stirring occasionally. Once the mixture starts to bubble around the edges, remove from heat. Allow to cool for 10 minutes.
3. In a separate bowl, whisk together the egg yolks, flour, and salt. Temper the egg mixture by slowly whisking in a small portion of the hot milk mixture into the egg mixture.

4. Slowly add the remaining hot milk mixture to the egg mixture, whisking constantly until the mixture is even.

5. Heat the mixture over medium heat, stirring constantly, until it starts to thicken, about 7-10 minutes.

6. Remove the saucepan from heat and stir in the mashed avocado, vanilla extract, and salt.

7. Pour the custard into 4 ramekins.

8. Place the ramekins inside a larger baking dish and add enough hot water to come halfway up the sides of the ramekins.

9. Bake in a preheated oven at 350F for 45 minutes.

10. Allow the custards to cool before serving.

Nutrition Information:
Calories – 217, Total Fat – 8.6g, Saturated Fat – 3.4g, Cholesterol – 92mg, Sodium – 39mg, Total Carbohydrates – 29.1g, Dietary Fiber – 3.2g, Sugar – 23g, Protein – 5.3g.

83. Chocolate Chip Cookie Dough Custard

Revel in the deliciousness of this creamy, chocolate chip cookie dough custard. This rich and creamy custard, with an irresistible cookie dough flavor, is perfect for any day of the week!

Serving: 8-10 | Preparation Time: 35 minutes | Ready Time: 4 hours

Ingredients:
- 2 cups whole milk
- 1 cup heavy cream
- 2/3 cup sugar
- 2 tablespoons cornstarch
- 1/2 teaspoon salt
- 2 teaspoons pure vanilla extract
- 1 1/2 cups semi-sweet chocolate chips
- 1/2 cup butter, melted
- 1 1/2 cups chocolate chip cookie dough

Instructions:
1. In a small bowl, combine the cornstarch with 2 tablespoons of the milk and whisk until the mixture is lump-free.
2. In a medium saucepan, heat the remaining milk, cream, sugars, salt, and vanilla over medium heat, stirring constantly until it starts to steam.
3. Slowly pour in the cornstarch mixture and cook for about three minutes until the mixture has thickened and looks like pudding.
4. Remove from heat and add the melted butter, chocolate chips, and cookie dough, stirring until everything is combined and the cookie dough is in small pieces.
5. Pour the custard mixture into 8-10 individual containers and refrigerate for at least 4 hours before eating.

Nutrition Information: Per serving: 29g fat, 27g carbohydrates, 4g protein, 168 calories

84. Lavender Lemon Custard

A unique, floral twist on traditional custard, Lavender Lemon Custard is a creamy, subtly-sweetened dessert that is sure to please any palate.

Serving: 4 | Preparation Time: 15 minutes | Ready Time: 45 minutes

Ingredients:
- 2 cups heavy whipping cream
- 1 tablespoon of culinary lavender
- 4 large eggs
- 3/4 cup sugar
- 2 tablespoons grated lemon zest
- 1/4 teaspoon fine sea salt
- 2 tablespoons fresh lemon juice

Instruction:
1. Preheat oven to 325F. Grease a 9-inch pie plate with butter.
2. In a medium saucepan, bring the cream and lavender to a boil over medium heat. Remove from heat, cover, and steep 15 minutes.
3. In a large bowl, whisk together the eggs, sugar, salt, lemon zest, and lemon juice until smooth.

4. Strain the cream to discard the lavender, and whisk into the egg mixture.
5. Pour into the prepared pie plate, and bake until custard is set, about 45 minutes.
6. Cool completely before serving.

Nutrition Information:
Calories: 315, Fat: 22g, Carbohydrates: 21g, Protein: 7g, Cholesterol: 173mg, Sodium: 126mg, Potassium: 133mg.

85. Angel Food Cake Custard

Angel Food Cake Custard is a light and sweet dessert ideal for ending a meal with a pleasant, creamy finish. With a luscious texture, it's a comforting and simple treat that anyone can enjoy.

Serving: 6 | Preparation Time: 10 minutes | Ready Time: 3+ hours

Ingredients:
- 3/4 cup sugar
- 3/4 cup all-purpose flour
- 1/4 teaspoon salt
- 6 egg whites
- 1 teaspoon vanilla extract
- 2 cups cold heavy cream

Instructions:
1. Preheat oven to 350 degrees F. Grease a 9-inch 10-cup tube pan.
2. In a medium bowl, whisk together the sugar, flour, and salt.
3. In a large bowl, using a hand mixer, beat the egg whites until stiff peaks are formed.
4. With the mixer running, slowly add the sugar mixture, a tablespoon at a time, until fully combined.
5. Add the vanilla extract and beat until just combined.
6. Pour the batter into the prepared pan and bake for 25-30 minutes, or until golden brown.
7. Let cool completely.

8. In a large bowl, whisk together the cream until it reaches stiff peaks.
9. Gently fold the cream into the cooled cake batter.
10. Pour the mixture into the prepared pan.
11. Cover and refrigerate for at least 3 hours before serving.

Nutrition Information: Calories 387 | Total Fat 24g | Sodium 247mg | Total Carbohydrate 37g | Protein 4g

86. Salted Caramal Creme Bralee Custard

This salted caramel custard is a sweet and salty dessert made with a lot of creamy custard and a salted caramel topping. The crunchy, sweet and salty flavours make it a great dessert for any occasion.

Serving: 8 | Preparation Time: 15 minutes | Ready Time: 1 hour

Ingredients:
- 2 cups of whole milk
- 3 tablespoons of all-purpose flour
- 2 egg yolks
- 1/2 cup of white sugar
- 1/3 cup of granulated sugar
- 1 teaspoon of salt
- 1/4 cup of butter
- 1 cup of heavy cream
- 1 teaspoon of vanilla extract
- 1/4 cup of store-bought salted caramel sauce

Instructions:
1. Preheat oven to 350F.
2. In a medium-sized bowl, whisk together the milk, flour, and egg yolks until combined and smooth.
3. In a separate bowl, mix together the sugars and salt.
4. In a medium saucepan over medium-high heat, melt the butter and then add the sugar mixture, stirring until everything is combined.
5. Add the milk mixture and the cream, stirring constantly until the mixture begins to thicken slightly.
6. Remove the saucepan from the heat and stir in vanilla extract.

7. Pour the custard into a 9-inch pie dish and bake in preheated oven for 45 minutes, or until a knife inserted into the middle comes out clean.
8. Allow custard to cool for 15 minutes and then top with salted caramel sauce.

Nutrition Information: Per serving (1/8 of the recipe): Calories: 401; Total Fat: 19.2g; Saturated Fat: 10.4g; Trans Fat: 0.1g; Cholesterol: 104mg; Sodium: 361mg; Total Carbohydrate: 50.7g; Dietary Fiber: 0.1g; Sugars: 38.5g; Protein: 7.3g.

87. Honeycomb Custard

Honeycomb Custard is an easy to make, delicious dessert that pairs crunchy crunchy honeycomb with a creamy custard. It is the perfect comfort food to share with friends and family during a get together or just to indulge in yourself.

Serving: 8 | Preparation Time: 20 minutes | Ready Time: 4 hours

Ingredients:
- 500 mL each of whole milk and double cream
- 6 large eggs
- 140 g caster sugar
- 1 teaspoon vanilla extract
- 120 g honeycomb bars, broken into pieces

Instructions:
1. In a bowl, whisk together the eggs, sugar, and vanilla extract until light and creamy.
2. Heat the milk and cream in a saucepan over medium heat until small bubbles just start to appear around the edges.
3. Slowly pour the hot milk and cream into the egg mixture, whisking constantly.
4. Pour the mixture back into the saucepan and cook for about 5 minutes over medium heat, stirring regularly.
5. Pour the custard mixture into 8 small ramekins.
6. Sprinkle the honeycomb pieces over the custard.

7. Place the ramekins on a baking dish. Add enough hot water to the dish to come halfway up the sides of the ramekins.
8. Bake in a preheated oven (170°C) for 45 minutes.
9. Cool in the refrigerator for 4 hours or overnight.

Nutrition Information:
Per Serving (1/8) – Calories: 291 kcal, Carbohydrates: 22.7 g, Protein: 8.7 g, Fat: 17.1 g, Cholesterol: 144 mg, Sodium: 71 mg, Fiber: 0.2 g, Sugar: 12.7 g, Vitamin D: 14.7 mcg, Calcium: 151.7 mg, Iron: 0.7 mg.

88. Churro Custard

Churro Custard is a rich and creamy Spanish-inspired dessert. It combines the unforgettable taste of cinnamon sugar-dusted churros with a luxurious custard filling. This delightful treat is an ideal way to satisfy everyone's sweet tooth.

Serving: 8-10 | Preparation Time: 10 minutes | Ready Time: 2.5 hours

Ingredients:
• 2 cups milk
• 2 cups heavy cream
• 5 large eggs
• 2/3 cup granulated sugar
• 2 teaspoons vanilla extract
• 1 teaspoon ground cinnamon
• 2 tablespoons brown sugar
• 1/2 teaspoon ground nutmeg
• vegetable oil, for deep-frying
• 3/4 cup all-purpose flour
• 1 teaspoon salt

Instructions:
1. In a medium saucepan, heat the milk and cream over low heat until it is just steaming.
2. In a separate bowl, whisk together the eggs, sugar, and vanilla extract until well combined.

3. Slowly pour the milk and cream mixture into the egg mixture, whisking constantly.

4. Add the cinnamon, nutmeg, and brown sugar and whisk until evenly combined.

5. Pour the custard mixture into a large baking dish and cover with foil. Place in a larger baking dish and fill the larger dish with 1 inch of hot water.

6. Bake for 1 1/2 hours. The custard should be slightly firm when done.

7. Meanwhile, heat enough vegetable oil in a medium saucepan to hit a depth of 3-inches.

8. In another medium bowl, whisk together the flour and salt. Gradually add 1 3/4 cups water to make a thick batter.

9. Once the oil is hot, use a spoon to carefully drop spoonfuls of batter into the hot oil. Fry until golden brown, about 1 minute.

10. Remove the churros with a slotted spoon and drain on a paper towel-lined plate.

11. Sprinkle the drained churros with cinnamon sugar.

12. Once the custard is finished baking, remove from the oven and let cool for 30 minutes.

13. Place the cooled custard into individual serving dishes and top with a churro.

Nutrition Information:
Calories: 420, Fat: 32 g, Protein: 5 g, Carbohydrates: 22 g, Fiber: 1 g, Cholesterol: 110 mg, Sodium: 280 mg.

89. Peaches and Cream Custard

This Peaches and Cream Custard is a delicious combination of creamy custard and sweet and juicy peaches, perfect for any special occasion.

Serving: 8-10 | Preparation Time: 15 minutes | Ready Time: 1 hour

Ingredients:
• 4 1/2 cups of heavy cream
• 3 large eggs
• 1/4 cup granulated sugar
• 2 teaspoons of vanilla extract

• 2 cups of canned peach slices
• 1 tablespoon of Powdered sugar

Instructions:
1. Pre-heat the oven to 350degrees Fahrenheit.
2. In a medium sized bowl, whisk together the heavy cream, eggs, sugar, and vanilla extract until well blended.
3. Place the peach slices in the bottom of a 9 x 13 inch baking dish.
4. Pour the cream mixture over the peach slices.
5. Bake in the oven for 40-45 minutes, or until the custard is just set in the center.
6. Allow to cool for 15 minutes, then sprinkle with powdered sugar to serve.

Nutrition Information:
Calories: 230 per serving
Fat: 15g
Carbohydrates: 15g
Protein: 8g

90. Chocolate Swirl Custard

Chocolate Swirl Custard is a luxurious dessert that is sure to mesmerize everyone's taste buds. This decadent treat brings together delicious custard, chocolate and sugar swirls, and an amazing chocolate finish.

Servings: 8 , | Preparation Time: 20 minutes, | Ready Time: 1 hour 30 minutes

Ingredients:
-3 cups of whole milk
-1/2 cup granulated sugar
-5 egg yolks
-3 tablespoons cornstarch
-1/4 teaspoon salt
-1 teaspoon pure vanilla extract
-1/2 cup condensed milk
-2 ounces melted semi-sweet chocolate chips

Instructions:
1. In a medium-sized saucepan, heat the milk, sugar, and salt over medium heat. Stir consistently until the sugar dissolves, about 4 minutes.
2. In a small bowl, whisk together the egg yolks and cornstarch. Gradually pour a small amount of the heated milk into the egg yolk mixture and whisk vigorously.
3. Slowly pour the egg mixture back into the saucepan and whisk constantly for about 8 minutes until the custard thickens and coats the back of the spoon.
4. Remove the saucepan from the heat and add the vanilla extract and condensed milk. Stir until fully combined.
5. Divide the custard into 8 separate heatproof cups or small ramekins. Then, top the custard with 2 ounces of melted semi-sweet chocolate chips, swirling the chocolate into the custard with a spoon.
6. Place the cups into the refrigerator and allow the custard to chill and set for 1 hour.

Nutrition Information: Calories 177, Total Fat 8.3g, Saturated Fat 4.7g, Sodium 137mg, Carbohydrate 21.2g, Protein 4.9g.

91. Oreo Cookie Custard

Oreo Cookie Custard is an indulgent, rich and creamy dessert that is sure to become a family favourite.

Serving: Serves 6. | Preparation Time: 10 minutes | Ready Time: 1 hour 15 minutes

Ingredients:
- 6 Oreo cookies
- 2 Cups Heavy Cream
- 5 Egg Yolks
- 2/3 Cup Sugar
- 2 tsp Vanilla Extract

Instructions:
1. Preheat oven to 350F and break Oreo cookies into pieces. Spread the pieces on the bottom of an 8x8 inch baking dish, and set aside.

2. In a medium saucepan, combine the cream, egg yolks, and sugar. Cook over medium heat, stirring constantly, until the mixture thickens and coats the back of a spoon.

3. Remove the saucepan from the heat, and stir in the vanilla extract. Pour the mixture over the Oreo pieces in the baking dish.

4. Bake in preheated oven for 25-30 minutes or until the custard is set. Let cool completely before serving.

Nutrition Information:
Per Serving: 384 calories; 23.2 g fat; 31.9 g carbohydrates; 7.7 g protein; 103 mg cholesterol; 155 mg sodium.

92. Buttermilk Custard

Buttermilk Custard is a classic, comforting dessert perfect for any occasion. With just five easy ingredients and minimal mess, this custard is sure to become a favorite for both you and your guests.

Serving: 8 | Preparation Time: 10 minutes | Ready Time: 45 minutes

Ingredients:
- 21/2 cups buttermilk
- 1/4 cup granulated sugar
- 1/4 teaspoon kosher salt
- 3 large eggs
- 1 teaspoon pure vanilla extract

Instructions:
1. Preheat the oven to 325F. Grease an 8-inch round baking dish with butter and set aside.

2. In a medium bowl, whisk together the buttermilk, sugar, salt, eggs, and vanilla until thoroughly combined.

3. Pour the mixture into the prepared baking dish. Place the dish in the oven and bake for 40-45 minutes, until the custard is set and lightly golden around the edges.

4. Remove the custard from the oven and let cool for 10 minutes before serving. Enjoy!

Nutrition Information (per serving):
Calories: 142, Total Fat: 5 g, Saturated Fat: 2 g, Cholesterol: 79 mg, Sodium: 117 mg, Carbohydrate: 18 g, Protein: 6 g, Vitamin A: 7%, Vitamin C: 0%, Calcium: 20%, Iron: 2%

93. Coffee and Donut Custard

Coffee and Donut Custard is a delicious and easy to make dessert that combines the flavors of coffee, donuts, and custard. This creamy and flavorful dessert is sure to be a hit with family and friends.

Serving: 8 | Preparation Time: 10 minutes | Ready Time: 5 minutes

Ingredients:
· 2 cups cold espresso coffee
· 1/2 cup whipped cream
· 1/2 cup all-purpose flour
· 2 tablespoons granulated sugar
· 2 tablespoons butter, softened
· 4 large eggs
· 1/2 teaspoon ground cinnamon
· 4 cups confectioners' sugar
· 1 teaspoon salt
· 1 cup heavy cream
· 6 baked glazed donuts, chopped

Instructions:
1. Preheat oven to 350 degrees.
2. In a medium bowl, whisk together espresso, whipped cream, flour, sugar, butter, eggs, and cinnamon.
3. Stir in 1 cup of the confectioners' sugar, salt and heavy cream until well blended.
4. Spread the mixture into a lightly greased 9x13-inch baking dish.
5. Sprinkle chopped donuts over the custard and push lightly into the custard.
6. Bake in the preheated oven for 35-40 minutes or until lightly golden and set.
7. Let cool and dust with remaining confectioners' sugar.

Nutrition Information:
Serving size: 1/8 of the dish
Calories: 390
Fat: 19 g
Carbohydrates: 50 g
Protein: 6 g

94. Blueberry Cheesecake Custard

This stunning Blueberry Cheesecake Custard will make the perfect summer dessert for any occasion! With its silky-smooth texture and delicate sweetness, it's an easy and delicious no-bake treat that your whole family will love.

Serving: 8 | Preparation Time: 10 minutes | Ready Time: 2 hours

Ingredients:
- 8 ounces cream cheese, softened
- 2 1/2 cups blueberries
- 1 cup granulated sugar
- 2 tablespoons cornstarch
- 2 tablespoons fresh lemon juice
- 1/2 teaspoon lemon zest
- 1/2 teaspoon ground cinnamon
- 1/4 teaspoon salt
- 2 cups whole milk
- 1/2 cup heavy cream

Instructions:
1. In a medium bowl, beat cream cheese and sugar with an electric mixer until light and fluffy.
2. In a separate bowl, mix together cornstarch, lemon juice, lemon zest, cinnamon, and salt.
3. In a medium saucepan, combine blueberries, sugar, cornstarch mixture, and milk. Cook over medium heat, stirring constantly, until mixture starts to thicken.
4. Remove from heat and stir in heavy cream.

5. Pour mixture into a 9-inch pie plate and spread cheesecake mixture evenly over the top.
6. Preheat oven to 350F and bake for 25-30 minutes or until top is lightly browned.
7. Cool completely before serving.

Nutrition Information:
Calories: 203, Total Fat: 9.5 g, Total Carbohydrates: 27.2 g, Protein: 4.1 g, Sodium: 148 mg, Cholesterol: 24 mg

95. Mint Chocolate Chip Custard

Mint Chocolate Chip Custard: Deliciously creamy and full of flavor, this Mint Chocolate Chip Custard is a must-try dessert! Sure to satisfy any sweet tooth, you'll be sure to impress your friends and family with this one!

Serving: 6 | Preparation Time: 15 minutes | Ready Time: 1 hour

Ingredients:
- 2 cups heavy cream
- 2 cups whole milk
- 6 egg yolks
- 1/2 cup plus 2 tablespoons granulated sugar
- 1/2 teaspoon salt
- 4 teaspoons peppermint extract
- 3/4 teaspoon pure vanilla extract
- 12 ounces semi-sweet chocolate chips

Instructions:
1. Preheat oven to 325 degrees F.
2. In a medium saucepan, warm the cream and milk over medium heat until almost boiling.
3. In a large bowl, whisk together the egg yolks, sugar, and salt. Slowly pour the warm cream and milk into the egg yolk mixture, whisking constantly.
4. Add the peppermint and vanilla extract, and whisk until combined.
5. Strain the custard mixture through a fine mesh sieve into a large bowl.

6. Place six 6-ounce oven safe ramekins or custard cups into a shallow roasting pan. Divide the custard among the ramekins and sprinkle chocolate chips over each one.
7. Place the roasting pan with the filled ramekins in the preheated oven. Carefully pour hot water into the roasting pan until it comes halfway up the sides of the ramekins.
8. Bake for 25 minutes, or until the custards are set.
9. Remove the ramekins from the roasting pan and let cool for 10 minutes before serving.

Nutrition Information:
Calories: 464; Fat: 28.6g; Cholesterol: 179mg; Sodium: 213mg; Protein: 6.4g; Carbohydrates: 47.7g; Sugar: 36.2g

96. Strawberry Cheesecake Custard

This strawberry cheesecake custard is a creamy and dreamy dessert that is sure to please. Bursting with the sweetness of strawberries and the richness of cream cheese, this custard is sure to delight.

Serving: 4-6 | Preparation Time: 10 min | Ready Time: 50 min

Ingredients:
-200g cream cheese
-500ml of double cream
-1/2 teaspoon of vanilla extract
-1/4 cup of sugar
-3 eggs
-50g of white chocolate chips
-1/2 cup of fresh strawberries, diced
-3 tablespoons of biscuit crumbs

Instructions:
1. Preheat the oven to 350F/180°C.
2. In a bowl, mix together cream cheese, double cream, sugar, eggs and vanilla extract until blended.

3. Grease an 8-inch round cake tin with butter and sprinkle the biscuit crumbs on the base.

4. Pour the cheesecake batter into the tin and sprinkle the white chocolate chips and strawberries over the top.

5. Bake for 45-50 minutes, until the custard is firm and golden-brown. Allow to cool and serve.

Nutrition Information: Per serving – Calories: 376, Total Fat: 24g, Saturated Fat: 13g, Cholesterol: 163mg, Sodium: 219mg, Carbohydrates: 30g, Fiber: 1g, Sugar: 17g, Protein: 7g

97. Chocalate Soufale Custard

Chocolate Souffle Custard is a delicious and indulgent dessert that combines the flavors of rich dark chocolate with a decadent creamy texture. It is the perfect ending to any special meal and is sure to make any guest feel pampered.

Serving: 4-6 | Preparation Time: 15 minutes | Ready in:1 hour

Ingredients:
* 4 ounces semi-sweet chocolate chips
* 2 tablespoons cocoa powder
* 1/4 cup sugar
* 2 egg yolks
* 1/4 cup heavy cream
* 1/4 teaspoon vanilla extract
* 1/4 cup butter (Optional)

Instructions:
1. Preheat oven to 350 degrees.
2. Combine the chocolate chips, cocoa powder and sugar in a medium heatproof bowl.
3. In a separate bowl, whisk together the egg yolks, cream, and vanilla until combined.
4. Pour the cream mixture into the chocolate mixture and stir to combine.

5. If using butter, add it to the mixture and stir until completely combined.
6. Pour the mixture into 4-6 individual ovenproof dishes.
7. Bake for 20 minutes or until set. Let cool.

Nutrition Information:
Serving Size: 1,
Calories: 250,
Total Fat: 17 g,
Cholesterol: 83 mg,
Sodium: 108 mg,
Total Carbohydrates: 19 g,
Protein: 5 g.

CONCLUSION

Custard is an incredibly delicious dessert that is versatile enough to be used in a wide range of recipes. This cookbook offers 97 mouth-watering recipes that showcase the unique and delightful flavors of custard. From baked custards, custard tarts, custard mousses, custard ice creams, and classic creme brulee to more creative recipes like chili-custard bread and strawberry-custard s'mores, this cookbook has something for everyone and every occasion.

With each recipe, the cookbook offers clear, easy-to-follow steps and helpful tips to ensure that your custard creation tastes perfect. There are a variety of ingredients and flavors that can be used to customize each recipe, and the book even provides ideas to accommodate those with allergic reactions or dietary restrictions.

This cookbook provides a great way to explore and expand your baking repertoire and will add a special and unique touch to your desserts. The 97 delicious custard recipes are sure to please everyone's taste buds and are guaranteed to be a hit at any function. Whether you're hosting a big get-together or just showing off your baking skills at home, these recipes will have your guests talking. So grab your apron, preheat the oven, and get ready to enjoy some of the sweetest treats you've ever tasted. Enjoy and bon appetit!